9545

# The English Cat at Home

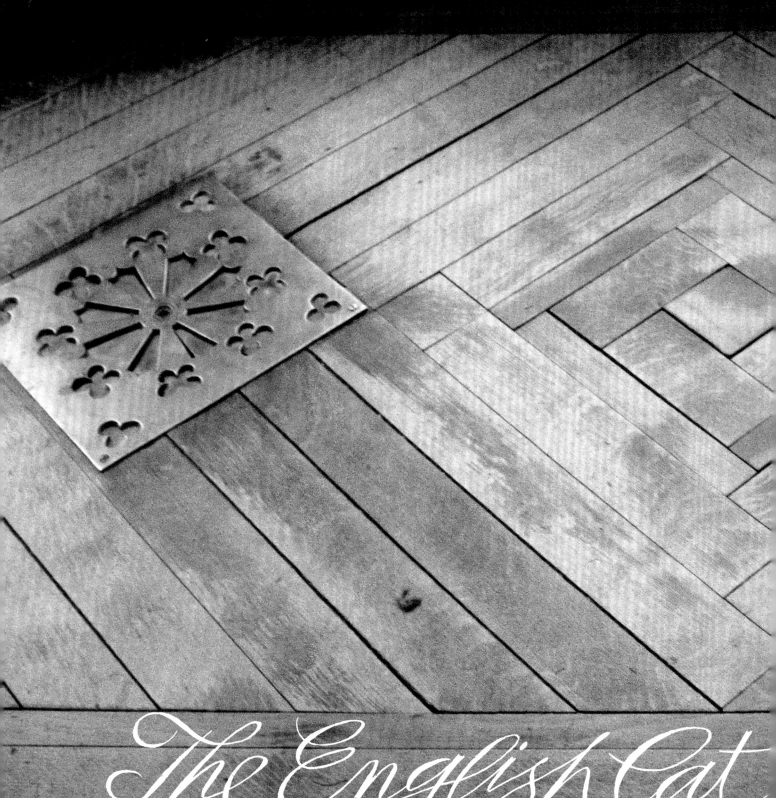

The English Cat

# at Home

Matthew Sturgis / Photographs by Toby Glanville
Salem House · Topsfield, Massachusetts

First published in the United States
by Salem House Publishers, 1989.
462 Boston Street
Topsfield, MA 01983

Pawprints by Tizzy

ISBN 0 88162 402 0

Printed in Great Britain

Front endpaper: Caroline Colthurst's kitten, Little Lucifer
Title page: One of Mr and Mrs John McClintock's eight cats
Page 6: Caroline Colthurst's brown Burmese, Nishko
Page 9: The Hon. Hector MacDonnell's cat, Minou
Page 160: One of Lady Abdy's two blue-cream Persians
Back endpaper: One of David Vicary's six cats

# Contents

ACKNOWLEDGEMENTS

We owe a great debt of thanks to all the cats and owners who appear in these pages, for their patience, kindness and hospitality. And also to Flora McDonnell, Sir Roger and Lady Young, Gregor and Kate Murray, Rebecca Nicolson, Tim Bishop and Robin Flower.

M.H.S. and T.G.

FOR LILY

# Sarah Snow

'Cats are only human, they have their faults,' says Kingsley Amis. 'You don't pick your friends because of their virtues, but you put up with them being boring if they put up with you.' Kingsley puts up with his cat Sarah Snow – and Sarah puts up with Kingsley. Indeed, they are very good friends. 'I like cats more than most people like cats. They give me violent hay-fever. I have a sneezing fit each morning. If it wasn't for Sarah I could go without a handkerchief.'

Sarah is a beautiful and slender, long-haired, white cat with pale green eyes and a pink nose. Sarah is almost twelve years old. 'She's English, you know,' Kingsley insists. 'Nothing fancy. I don't really like exotic cats. They can be pretty, but people who say they are highly-strung are quite right.'

Sarah herself is extremely pretty and positively low-strung. She likes almost nothing so much as dozing next to the radiator behind the sofa in Kingsley's bedroom. Sarah, as her name reveals, is a female; Kingsley, in spite of some of his literary critics, prefers females. 'I always like to have female animals – they're nicer and gentler.' Nevertheless, 'Sarah is a ruddy pest in some ways.' One of her most vexing habits, in Kingsley's view, is greeting him each morning with a hideous yowling noise: a cry suggesting that he has just trodden upon her tail but, in fact, intimating that she is glad to see him and now wants her breakfast.

Nor is this Sarah's only fault. 'She has an instinct for going into holes. She once got behind the skirting board at a friend's house.' Invariably she emerges from her pot-holing expeditions covered in filth, all too noticeable on a white cat; and she does not scruple to shed the dirt all over the house. She does, however, have some instincts – albeit misguided – for personal cleanliness. 'One daren't leave the bathroom door open as Sarah thinks the shower was created for her convenience.' Even putting her out into the garden creates its problems. 'She has got no sense of finding her way back in after she's been let out.' She is forever on the wrong side of the door.

Kingsley has considered cutting a hole for the cat in his study door, not only because Sarah likes to come and sit on his lap while he is working, but also because of an account he had recently heard about Issac Newton and his cat. Newton had a cat of which he was very fond. She would, however, annoy him by disturbing his studies with demands to be let in (or out of) the room. To ease life for both the cat and himself, Newton had a cat-sized hole cut in the bottom of the door. The scheme was a great success and when his cat produced a kitten Newton summoned the carpenter again and got him to cut a kitten-sized aperture beside the first hole. Kingsley is delighted to think that the genius who mapped out the limits of our universe failed to grasp that a kitten could fit through a cat-sized hole.

But then, as Kingsley remarks, 'People are silly about their cats.' Kingsley is very fond of Sarah and Sarah is very fond of him. 'She is also very friendly with strangers. She sits outside on the wall at the front of the house and stops people in the street.' She is so attentive to visitors that some of them have been led to suspect that Kingsley doesn't give her enough affection. 'It couldn't be less true,' he says.

Although, as all cat-lovers do, Kingsley has reservations about the feline habit of extending claws into one's leg when sitting on one's knee, he spends a lot of time stroking Sarah. 'There is no doubt that it is very flattering when a cat jumps on to your lap.'

Cats not only flatter their owners, they also amuse them. Kingsley delights in Sarah's antics, and the solemn expression she wears as she performs them. 'Cats are very straight-faced,' he says, before adding, 'Obviously they can't really smile. It would be terrifying if they could.' He also takes particular pleasure in cats that can raid fridges. He sees this as a fine sign of feline intelligence. He has a high regard for their cleverness. 'Cats aren't as stupid as they often seem,' he says. Sarah stares innocently out of the window.

Kingsley Amis has always lived among pets. Although as a child his family kept only dogs, ever since he married he has had both cats and dogs. Now, however, he just has Sarah. 'I'd love to have a dog too,' he confesses, 'but I can't exercise one here.' He cherishes an affection for Alsatians, not the breed best-suited to life in a London flat. Keeping pets is important. 'I am enough of a cat-lover,' admits Kingsley, 'to be suspicious of a household that doesn't have a cat – especially if they don't have a dog either. I associate a person having a cat with them being gentler than other people.'

Pets can also tinge their owners with poetry. 'There is no point in having a cat and being prosaic about it. Cats stimulate the fancy; we weave fantasies about them. But it's like politics – people will always go further than you would like. Those awful cat postcards and statuettes! It is very hard to draw the line.' Kingsley is uncertain quite where he draws the line. He talks to Sarah a lot and has even written a poem about their conversation. 'I say a lot of silly things to Sarah – and about her,' says Kingsley. Sometimes he even employs her as an imaginary secretary, signing letters to irksome correspondents with her name, p.p. Kingsley Amis.

'I have an occasional urge,' he confesses, 'to write a story about an old man and his cat . . .' In the story the old man is something of a drinker and each evening, as he reaches for the gin bottle, he always asks his big black cat, 'What about a drink for you, Puss?' And, getting no reply, he berates the animal for being such poor fun.

One night, however, much to his amazement, the jesting question is answered. 'Yes, please. I should love a drink,' the cat replies. They drink a toast, and then another. They get drunk together, talking of old times, and end by dancing a jig in front of the dying embers. The next morning the man wakes with a not unfamiliar headache. But, seeing the cat, he remembers the jollity of the night before and chaffs the cat about the fine time they had of it. The cat stares blankly at him, before narrowing its eyes and turning to look at the sun. The man, with a sense of panic, supposes that he has imagined the whole episode; his mind must be softening. He returns to bed in despair. When the cleaning lady comes by she is quite put out by the mess. Under the sofa there are two empty tumblers. One of them, she notes with disgust, has some black hairs on the rim.

I turned to Sarah to get her reaction to the story but she just stared blankly at me, before narrowing her eyes and turning to look at the sun.

# Mr Toddy

Mice are fecund, foolish and fond of malted grain. This is good news for young Mr Toddy and bad news for the mouse population of Glenturret. Mr Toddy is the new official mouse catcher at the very picturesque and equally distinguished Glenturret distillery.

It is an impressive tribute to the mouse-ish characteristics mentioned above that there is still a mouse population of Glenturret to keep in check, because for nearly twenty-four years (from April 1963 to March 1987) the Glenturret distillery was the home, and employer, of the prodigious Towser: Towser the world's greatest mouser. During her long life Towser killed some 28,899 mice, an average of almost three a day, a feat of wholesale slaughter that earned her a place in the *Guinness Book of Records*. Mr Toddy has to follow this difficult act.

Towser has become a part of Scottish folk history, appearing in American magazines, Japanese television programmes and books as distinguished as this one. Each year she received hundreds of letters from all over the world. She has entered the pantheon of Scottish national celebrities, a feline companion to Greyfriars' Bobby. Indeed a children's story tape recounting the tales of Towser and Bobby has been produced and, so I was told, is one of the diversions of the royal nursery.

Towser, of course, was not unused to royal interest. Although, despite her longevity, she never received a royal telegram, she did get a letter from the Palace on her twenty-first birthday. By chance she shared her natal day with the Queen an occasion celebrated each year at Glenturret with a large cake decorated with sugar mice. Towser would take time off from the fray to pose beside this confection and receive admirers with the easy grace of a natural star and a cat-of-action.

When Towser died at the beginning of 1987 she left a great gap not only in the affections of the people of Glenturret but also in the defences of the distillery's grain store. A competition was held with all due speed to find a replacement. Towser had been spayed and had no offspring. The contest, keen and close, was between a young lion cub, a small chimpanzee and two stray kittens, brothers, provided by the Scottish Society for the Prevention of Cruelty to Animals. In the event, Mr Toddy impressed most with his energy, speed and agility. He was selected as Towser's heir, the distillery accountant took Mr Toddy's brother, Hamish, and the other two contestants were returned, disappointed, to the local wildlife park.

It is not uncommon for pets to come to resemble their masters

but for a cat to take on the look of a place is perhaps rare. Not only has Mr Toddy the name of a whisky cat; he also has the features of one. The lights and darks of his sleek, brown tabby coat are flecked with white, rippling like the peaty flood of the River Turret that runs briskly under the distillery walls. Although his thick, ringed tail does not lend itself easily to a distillery analogy, having more of the raccoon about it than the tun-room, his eyes are pure whisky. They have the liquid golden depths of a prize-winning 21-year-old malt; they sparkle with candour, curiosity and intelligence. Mr Toddy is a darling cat.

When we met him, he had been at Glenturret for only six weeks but had already caught several mice and charmed the distillery employees, as well as the many tourists who visit the place. The distillery, Scotland's oldest, is a collection of low white-washed buildings nestling in a curve of the River Turret, near Crieff in

Perthshire. (The water from the river is merely used for cooling. They pipe the whisky water from Loch Turret at the head of the glen.) It is surrounded by lush Perthshire fields, fields swarming with field mice who are attracted to the distillery by the temptingly stacked sacks of malted barley in the malt store.

Towser, regarding attack as the best form of defence, had carried his crusade out into the fields. He is now buried near to his favourite hunting ground, on the hill above the distillery by the large tank where the water from the loch is stored for easy use. As yet, young Mr Toddy confines his own patrols to the immediate area of the distillery, the malt store, the still-room and the tun-room. He sleeps in the still-room, where the air is warm and thick with whisky. (Towser's long life was generally ascribed to the amounts of the 'water of life' she had imbibed through breathing in the whisky-heavy atmosphere of the place.) Although Mr Toddy has a bed made from an empty whisky box, with typical feline perversity he prefers to sleep in the narrow, cosy space between two spirit tanks.

He is being trained up to his career by his minder (and admirer) Rena Steel. He has a golfball to practise his chasing with and he is on the sort of diet that Olympic rowing crews hope to receive: minced beef, chicken, fish, milk – fortified sometimes with a raw egg and sometimes with a wee dram. Mr Toddy, with his heavy paws and large ears, is certainly a natural hunter. He executes elaborate stalking manoeuvres, darting for cover, then hugging close to the walls of a distillery building before pouncing with great gusto upon his imaginary prey. One wonders whether the small chimpanzee would have shown either such diligence or such grace. The twin forces of nature and nurture are conspiring happily to produce a worthy successor to Towser.

Like his predecessor, Mr Toddy has a very amiable disposition. He loves people and is not at all bashful about either giving or receiving affection. He divides much of his time between welcoming trippers to the distillery, keeping an eye on them as they make their tour, and sitting in the warmth of the staffroom soaking up the attention; he is, after all, an important member of the staff himself.

By happy coincidence Mr Toddy's birthday is reckoned to fall, like Towser's and the Queen's, on 21 April, so the annual party can continue unchanged, celebrating the fame of Glenturret's great whisky chasers.

# Minou

Cats are untroubled by false modesty when contemplating their own charm and good looks. Minou knows that she is gorgeous and, while not making a vulgar show of it, expects adoration as her due. Minou, however, does not have a monopoly on charm and good looks; she must share her own abundance of these characteristics with her master, the Hon. Hector MacDonnell, painter, Irish folklorist and antiquarian. There is an affectionate rivalry between them. Nevertheless, while Hector does have some very fine jackets they must struggle to match the harlequin-splendour of Minou's coat, thick and fluffy in bold checks of white and tortoise-shell with matching plus-fours and smart white stockings.

Minou was very nearly called Grippe. She arrived as a kitten some three years ago, just as Hector was struck down by a bout of influenza. His perception was somewhat dominated by his illness and he thought Grippe might be a suitable name. Luckily his aunt intervened and declared that the cat should be called Minou, since all French cats are called Minou. No one thought to point out that the kitten was not French but Welsh. All cats, after all, have a certain Frenchness – a *je ne sais quoi* – about them.

Minou, though born on a Welsh farm, now divides her life between Ireland and Chelsea. We visited her and Hector at Glenarm where they live in an old mill house down the road from the castle where Hector was brought up. The house is full of pictures and beds: Hector's passions. The living-room is largely taken up with a huge four-poster, a piece of furniture awaiting Hector's removal to a large but dilapidated old rectory nearby. Upstairs in Hector's bedroom-cum-studio there is a small, country four-poster decked with pretty curtains and, lest one's levée should prove too exhausting, there is also a conveniently-placed Russian day-bed by the window. While Minou shares Hector's pleasure in the horizontal mode, she is less taken with his passion for paint.

On one occasion she sat in the cadmium yellow, an error she compounded by clambering into bed with Hector. Hector, half asleep between the sheets, was entirely unaware of the diaster. As Minou snuggled up against him, her whole body was transformed into a giant paintbrush. In the morning Hector thought with horror that he must have been struck by some particularly virulent strain of jaundice. Then he noticed, to his relief, that the carpet and the bedspread had contracted the same ailment. He was able to follow the yellow trail to the sorrowful-looking Minou. He had to shave off some of her beautiful hair to free her from the yellow peril. It was

not a pleasant experience for either of them and Minou now keeps her distance from Hector's palette.

Minou's wariness of paint in no way diminished her affection for painters. She made firm friends with Hector's late mother, the painter and sculptor Angela Antrim. 'Typically, my mother professed to hate cats. This was totally untrue. She was once discovered stroking Minou with her soft hairbrush. But she delighted in saying, "This animal is taking a fancy to me; what's going to happen to it when I'm dead."' Minou has survived that sad event but Hector suspects that the cat may have taken on some of his mother's characteristics – her aristocratic bearing, her expectation of affection, her sense of mischief.

Such mystic resonances do not surprise Hector; Minou did arrive, perhaps significantly, during a partial eclipse of the sun. Moreover Hector is no stranger to the feline affinity for the supernatural; he was haunted by the ghost of his childhood cat, a female Siamese

This poem, decorated with pictures of Minou by Hector, was written by an Irish monk living in Germany in the ninth century. Although the author, like Hector, was Irish, his cat, to judge by its name, was, like Minou, Welsh.

PANGUR BAN

*I and Pangur Bán my cat*
*'Tis a like task we are at;*
*Hunting mice is his delight*
*Hunting words I sit all night.*

*Better far than praise of men*
*'Tis to sit with book and pen;*
*Pangur bears me no ill will,*
*He too plies his simple skill.*

*'Tis a merry thing to see*
*At our tasks how glad are we,*
*When at home we sit and find*
*Entertainment to our mind.*

*Oftentimes a mouse will stray*
*In our hero's, Pangur's, way;*
*Oftentimes my keen thought set*
*Takes a meaning in its net.*

*'Gainst the wall he sets his eye*
*Full and fierce and sharp and sly;*
*'Gainst the wall of knowledge I*
*All my little wisdom try.*

*When a mouse darts from its den,*
*O how glad is Pangur then!*
*O what gladness do I prove*
*When I solve the doubts I love.*

*So in peace our tasks we ply*
*Pangur Bán, my cat, and I;*
*In our arts we find our bliss,*
*I have mine and he has his.*

called Teddy. After Teddy's death her ghost would take up her former place at the end of Hector's bed. This continued for several months until her soul was freed from its torment and she disappeared to frolic for all eternity amongst the catnip that fringes the Elysian fields.

Minou's own frolics are confined to the glens of Antrim and the

gardens of Chelsea. She travels uncomplainingly between them, tolerating air travel and positively enjoying motor transport. 'She sits in the back of the car looking out at the traffic,' Hector explains. 'Or sometimes she will sit on my lap while I'm driving. I suppose I could be arrested as she doesn't wear a seatbelt.'

Minou also enjoys walking. She will accompany Hector on his strolls and, if he goes for an evening walk, she acts as an outrider, racing on ahead to check that the way is safe. She is much concerned with Hector's safety and well-being. Whenever he returns from travelling abroad she greets him with undisguised enthusiasm, demanding attention with kittenish playfulness. 'She has a cat-ball which she has consistently ignored since it was given to her, but when I return, in order to make a display of herself, she plays with it as though it were a mouse.'

Minou has a penchant for real mice too. She is a keen and stylish hunter. While there are mice aplenty in the fields and farmyards of Ireland, they are scarce in the streets of London, and Minou sometimes turns her attention to the birds. This is a dangerous course as one of Hector's Chelsea neighbours is a man who, unlikely as it seems, loves London pigeons. 'He is deeply antipathetic to cats,' says Hector. 'And is to be seen brandishing an air pistol. He has actually shot the tail off one cat.' Minou, however, has thus far escaped his unwelcome attentions. She continues to pursue her prey while her master pursues his art.

# Twilight

John Bratby has not always been a cat-lover. He admits that for most of his life he thought 'that people who went crazy over cats – or dogs – were feeble-minded.' And although during his first marriage there was a cat about the family's Blackheath home, he describes it as 'a solid, black, unattractive creature which wasn't taken much notice of.' John preferred goats. He used to have a goat called Billy with which he would wrestle. But Billy, as goats will be, was too mischievous and destructive and had to go. Time, however, and the second Mrs Bratby have mellowed John. The angry young man of Fifties' art, leader of the 'kitchen-sink' school of social realist painters, is now happy to pass the minutes dandling his new kitten, Twilight, on his lap, cajoling him with endearments.

Twilight, a tabby tom, whose pale-and-dark-striped flanks perhaps resemble the twilight sky, is a new arrival at the Cupola And The Four Winds, the Bratbys' rambling, timber-clad home, perched on a ridge overlooking Hastings. Splendid as the shambling house is, Twilight prefers the garden. For while the pepper-pot cupola may well be exposed to the rudeness of the four winds, the house itself is girdled by a succession of sheltered gardens, each plot upon a different level, each with a different flavour, from the well-domesticated lawn in front of the french windows, guarded by the effigies of two sacred Egyptian dogs, to the less kempt wilds of the orchard, along the northern wall of which stand three rough-hewn white thrones assembled from junk furniture and emblazoned with painted cockerels, creations that John undertook as a therapy and escape from painting.

Any cat would relish such a domain and Twilight skips with little shrieks of pleasure across the strips of lawn and amongst the tangled borders. John, an admirer of feline independence, is keen to teach Twilight the virtues of outdoor life, putting him out at night and spending time in the garden with him.

Sadly the studio is out of bounds. Paintings and palettes thick with bright and still wet colour are not happy companions for a frisky kitten. The scope for mess, destruction and impromptu abstract compositions of coloured paw-prints on the stair carpet is awesome.

At the moment, however, most of Twilight's creative energies are directed towards devising new wrestling throws for his catnip mouse. Mainly tabby, but with a handsome white beard (like his master), Twilight also has Siamese blood in his veins. The eastern strain shows itself in the soft, light-coloured fur of his stomach and

in his wide vocal range. Mercifully the plaintive home-sick wailing of his very early days with the Bratbys has given over almost entirely to little mews of pleasure and a soft insistent purr which starts up with happy ease.

John and Patti have had Twilight for only a few months. He was adopted after the death, at the age of seventeen, of Patti's beloved cat, Boots. There is a burial mound for Boots in one corner of the garden. It is constructed from bricks and ringed with catnip, some of which spills from earthenware pots shaped like primitive cats. Brightly coloured flowers adorn the memorial and over the whole stands one of John's mythic cockerels.

Boots converted John to cats. When he first met Patti (through a *Time Out* lonely hearts column) she was living with seven cats, a daunting prospect for any suitor, let alone one outside the ranks of cat-lovers. Patti, sensitive to the difficulty, got rid of five of her brood and, with scant enthusiasm, John accepted the remaining two cats – Boots and 'a big black one' – into his life.

He even had to accept Boots into his bed. Often Patti and he would be woken by the cat hurling herself against the bedroom door, thus opening it, and then bounding up on to the covers with a dead mouse or other trophy to be admired. He winces at the memory.

Despite these blood-stained nocturnal intrusions, John came, slowly, to love Boots. 'It goes hand in hand with my relationship with my wife, which,' he explains, 'has become more and more tender and considerate as the years pass. As I became softer towards Patti, I realized how much the cat meant to her. And I began to see it in a more affectionate manner. I began to be concerned about its feeding and comfort; I would talk to it. Quite out of character with my former self, I would put my forehead against its forehead.'

Nevertheless he still admits to some embarrassment at the endearments, soppy and touching, that Patti happily lavishes upon Twilight. But then he adds sagely. 'Of course I don't observe myself talking to the cat in the evenings . . .'

As a painter, John has always been alive to the aesthetic virtues of the cat family. He painted Boots several times; he looks forward to painting Twilight. 'Cats are beautiful creatures,' he says. 'From the aesthetic point of view, I think the cat family is amazingly beautiful. Although perhaps I prefer the look of lions and tigers.' But even the rambling gardens of the Cupola And The Four Winds might be a bit cramped for a lion. And what would the postman, who feeds the cat when the Bratbys are away, make of a tiger?

When John did do some lion paintings he had to hire models from a taxidermist. The results were not particularly happy, lacking the vitality and vigour that are so much a part of a big cat's beauty, and so much a part of John Bratby's best work.

Twilight, tirelessly bounding over the lawn and clambering eagerly over every friendly body, obviously shares some of his master's fabled energy – an energy that has fired John to paint an average of a picture a week throughout his working life.

Nevertheless, real and enthusiastic though John's affection for Twilight is, he still belongs to the ranks of those (perhaps rare in England) who think human beings are more important than animals. And, in the face of life's tragedies and troubles, he fears that he would be unable to turn for real comfort either to God or to Twilight. 'I don't believe in either of them – to that extent. Not yet, at least.'

# Miss Tabby Cat

Wightwick Manor is a Pre-Raphaelite gem. A richly-worked,
half-timbered house, it was built in the late 1880s from the profits
of Samuel Theodore Mander's paint factory, and decorated
throughout by Morris & Co. Its spacious rooms are thick with
Morris papers and hangings, with de Morgan tiles and W. A. S.
Benson chandeliers, with paintings and sketches by the
Pre-Raphaelite Brotherhood.

The house belongs to the National Trust; it is still lived in by
Lady Mander, the biographer and art historian, but it is run by
Miss Tabby Cat. Miss Tabby Cat is Lady Mander's forceful and
self-possessed puss. The reader will not be surprised to learn that
she is a tabby, female cat.

Miss Tabby Cat, Tabby to Lady Mander, is something of a
Pre-Raphaelite beauty herself. 'She is more a gamine than an
aristocrat,' says Lady Mander. Like not a few Pre-Raphaelite models
she was of lowly birth; she came from the gardener at the lodge.
Miss Tabby's languishing green eyes would have provoked the envy
of Jane Morris, while the striking yet elegant markings of her fur
might have inspired Rossetti's brush, and Burne-Jones could not but
have been moved by the expressive curve of her solemn mouth.
Miss Tabby's figure, however, would be more likely to call forth
the genius of a Rubens or a Renoir.

'Like a modern baby, she is fed on demand,' explains Lady
Mander. She is very demanding. During the course of our visit
Tabby asked for and consumed a great quantity of chopped liver.
Nor is food the only thing that Miss Tabby demands. She loves
adoration even more. In his foreword to Lady Mander's delightful
feline anthology, *CATegories*, A. L. Rowse states, with customary
audacity, that 'Cats are perfect writers' animals.' 'He couldn't be
more wrong,' says Lady Mander. 'Tabby only has to hear the
typewriter for her to appear at my desk, demanding to be stroked
or trying to sit on the keyboard.'

Miss Tabby Cat adopts similarly direct tactics to gain the
attention of visitors to the property. She has an instinct for taking
up positions where she is likely to make a large and memorable
impression – on a sumptuous chair, under a distinguished painting,
beside a well-stocked vase. Her favourite station, however, is on the
vast, dark red rug in the Great Parlour. Not only do the deep and
varied hues of the opulent weave provide a happy background for
her own rich colouring, but also the rug is graced with a large sign
forbidding visitors to walk on it. Tabby often seats herself directly

under this sign, flaunting her privilege and keeping a stern eye upon the passing parties.

The visitors, of course, adore her. In the splendidly-decorated Great Parlour, people are only too happy to turn away from good taste and high art and say, 'Look, there's a cat.' They say it as though they had never seen a cat before. Whole groups can abandon their tour-guide in front of Burne-Jones' magisterial *Love Among the Ruins*, to give their full attention to Miss Tabby Cat, licking her paws in the middle of the oriental rug. 'It rather throws some of our student guides,' says Lady Mander.

Miss Tabby, as well as her sense of mischief, has a keen appreciation of publicity. She was delighted when Wightwick Manor was chosen as the Victorian House for the *Treasure Houses of Britain* exhibition in Washington. And when an American film crew arrived to make the video for the exhibition, Tabby spent much of the time strolling deliberately into the picture and striking dramatic poses in the background while, to the fore, Lady Mander attempted to discuss the influence of Ruskin on late-Victorian wallpaper patterns. As a result Miss Tabby (and Lady Mander) now have a posse of transatlantic admirers.

Like all screen-stars Miss Tabby is keen to preserve some areas of privacy. The peril of seclusion is that one gets forgotten. On the rare occasions that Tabby has been locked in the library, she is found complaining loudly and sharpening her claws on the spines of some of the finer bindings. To save her from such distress, to preserve the book bindings and to prevent the cat setting off the burglar alarms, there is now a regular evening search for the said puss. Lady Mander and the caretaker chase round the house with saucers of chopped liver, calling the cat's name.

Even with the constricting limitations of the burglar-alarm system, Miss Tabby Cat still enjoys a large measure of freedom. She has constant access in and out of the house, via the wisteria and a cat-flap in the window of Lady Mander's bedroom. Although Tabby enjoys the gardens, with their mixture of the formal and the rough, the ordered grace of the golden holly walk and the wilder charms of the grass-fringed stream, she uses them more for leisure than for sport. Her hunting activity, never very engrossing, is now a minor sideline. There are better morsels to be had at Lady Mander's table.

Tabby has obviously taken to heart the lines of Herrick carved upon the oaken gable-ends at Wightwick:

'Live, live with me, and thou shalt see | The pleasures I'll prepare for thee:
What sweets the country can afford | Shall bless thy Bed and bless thy Board.'

# Fortnum & Mason

When Mr Fortnum established his grocery business in Piccadilly, he thought himself rather too grand to deal with the mundanities of stock-taking and cart unloading. So he took on a partner, Mr Mason, who was happy to handle the prosaic end of the business out in the back-yard amongst the tea chests, while he, Mr Fortnum, welcomed the duchesses at the door.

In similar fashion, Michael Parkin's cat Fortnum, a high-born grey-and-white, long-haired Russian, took on a partner from down the social scale. His Mr Mason is a sleek, well-muscled tabby from the alley (albeit the alley just behind Sloane Square).

Michael Parkin, the art dealer, got Fortnum (along with his impressive family-tree) over sixteen years ago when he still lived in Chelsea. Three days later Mason arrived unannounced and has stayed on ever since.

The two cats (both neutered toms) were inseparable from the start. They spent every night in each other's arms. 'They were a pair of old pooves,' recalls Michael affectionately. But Fortnum always remembered his breeding and Mason never forgot his place. Mason would do everything for Fortnum – clean him, save him food, give him the most comfortable bed. Fortnum was imperious in his demands to Michael. Tinned cat-food was not to be endured, and even fresh fish had to be of the finest. 'It was hake and halibut. "I don't want any of this cheap coley stuff," he would command.'

Sadly the above paragraph is all in the past tense because Fortnum died earlier this year, at the ripe age of sixteen. His spirit and image, however, live on. There is a fine double portrait of Fortnum and Mason by Nicolette Meers in the drawing-room at Michael's Norfolk home, Gunton Hall. It is a house full of beautiful feline images. There is a delightful mixture of style and tone, from the old painting of a fearsome ratter to the natty pictures of Louis Wain cats-about-town; from the photograph of Fortnum luxuriating upon a red-velvet cushion to the cover of the *Radio Times* with Mason perched upon Thérèse Raquin's lap.

There is also a more sombre memorial in the garden, Fortnum's gravestone, carved with his name and dates in Gill Sans. Mason visits the grave regularly, sitting upon it and contemplating his departed friend with stoic dignity.

Mason, even in the splendid surroundings of Gunton, has never lost touch with his commoner's roots. He has a streak of commonsense that will keep even his bereavement in proportion, unlike two of Michael's previous cats, Lytton and Carrington.

When Lytton was run over by a van it was all too, too much for poor Carrington. She was unable to face the future alone and pined completely away. A touching tale, but one that shows how careful one must be when choosing a cat's name.

Another of Michael's former cats was called Hodge – a name laden with Johnsonian gravitas one might think. But Hodge's chief delight was climbing the great plane trees in Berkeley Square. (Michael was then living in Mayfair.) Unfortunately Hodge's ability only reached to the ascent. He was wholly unable to climb down a tree. At first the fire-brigade were sympathetic but when Hodge, obviously impressed by their tree-top rescue service, persisted in his climbing activities they took to charging Michael for their time and effort.

As the bills arrived from the fire department, Hodge departed for the country. Michael reluctantly surrendered him to a rural friend. After the ordered pleasures of Mayfair, however, arcadia was incomprehensible to Hodge and he was eaten by a mad bull-mastiff.

Fortnum and Mason made the transition from town to country with less trauma. They moved from Chelsea to Norfolk four years ago and were quick to appreciate the amenity of Gunton Hall and its stately park. The hunting is excellent, the grounds spacious and the rooms well-proportioned.

Edward vii, like Fortnum and Mason, was much struck by the charm of the place and it is said that, in an effort financially to cripple the then owner, he paid several lengthy and expensive visits to the house, requiring lavish entertainments to be laid on and a special railway-station to be built. Such demands did almost ruin his unhappy host, and would certainly have done so had not a convnient 'fire' destroyed a small (and architecturally unimportant) part of the house, necessitating 'extensive repairs' and providing the owner with an excuse for avoiding further royal visitations. Edward vii admitted defeat and built Sandringham.

Gunton, having gradually fallen into decay, was recently rescued by the architect Kit Martin. He has ingeniously converted it into three palatial residences, one in the main body of the house and one in each wing. There are also several smaller apartments in the old servants' quarters at the back of the house. Mason lives in the West wing and is the senior cat on the estate. He takes an avuncular interest in Glentworth, Kit Martin's own young cat, which lives next door.

Mason, like his master, is a generous and attentive host. He loves visitors, and has the delightful habit of climbing on to their backs

and lying across their shoulders, an ever-warm and purring stole.
Even Sir John Rothenstein, who is not a cat-lover, has been won
over by Mason's displays of affection. It is impossible to ignore and
difficult to dislike a cat that springs nimbly on to your shoulder as
you enter a room and then lies there, happy to protect your neck
from draughts and soothe your brow with gentle purrs.

Michael has considered getting Mason a couple of kittens to be
the companions of his declining years ('They could be called Dixon
and Line,' he suggests), but Mason seems to be enjoying his
newly-acquired independence and might well resent the noisy
pranks of a hyperactive kitten. Moreover Michael sees himself and
his wife, Diana, as quite sufficient and suitable company for Mason.
Michael happily blurs the distinction between animals and
humans. He read *The Wind in the Willows* at an impressionable age
and now possesses a London telegraphic address listed as Toad Hall,
a sign warning weasels and stoats off his property, and a penchant
for loud check suits. His charming book of Louis Wain's cat
pictures is dedicated to 'My four cats, Fortnum and Mason, Sarah
and Sophie.' These last two are, in fact, his daughters.

Michael's association with Louis Wain, through exhibitions,
articles and books, has led to him being chosen as a judge for the
National Cat Club's Centenary Show. (Louis Wain designed the
club's coat-of-arms and wrote its motto, 'Beauty lives through
kindness'.) It is a happy sentiment and one that can cut both ways.
At Gunton the handsome Mason not only appreciates the Parkins'
affectionate care but he also breathes life and grace into their
elegant home by virtue of his own generous nature.

# Strayboy

To desert the metropolitan pleasures of Ebury Street for the ancient mysteries of a Bronze Age stone circle might not appeal to all. Indeed it might be beyond the fragile constitutions of many of us. But Pauline Flick and Strayboy are made of tougher stuff. They have renounced the well kempt fringes of Belgravia for the wind-blasted wilds of Great Rollright in Oxfordshire.

Pauline and Strayboy run a cat sanctuary there. Pauline is a rare spirit – a great cat-lover, author of a charming book *Christmas Cats*, and a keen admirer of Peter Shilton's goalkeeping. Strayboy is a much-battered but wholly unbowed tom cat, eccentrically marked in grey-tabby and white. They make a formidable pair.

When we visited them, there were fourteen cats in the sanctuary. Every colour (and numerous combinations) was represented in the crowd of cats that tumbled out of their out-house home to greet us. Tabbies, tortoiseshells, blacks, whites, black-and-whites, gingers and greys. In size they ranged from the well-set Strayboy, looking like a benevolent British ex-boxing champion who now runs a country hotel, to a small, fluffy-haired, black-and-white kitten whose manner, markings and condition suggested a tramp in evening dress. Their names speak for themselves: Fatty, Sandy, Jack (he's black) and Lazarus who returned from the dead having been savaged by a dog.

The cats all live together in one of the out-houses adjoining Pauline's gracious home. They have a large fenced area for their play, as the road runs very close to the house and Pauline has already lost one cat under the wheels of a passing motorcar. Jack and Leo live in the house with Pauline: Jack because he is rather cantankerous and Leo because she is so old. 'They all get on very well,' says Pauline. 'I have them all into the house to watch the television in the evening.'

Most of the cats come from a colony of strays that had gathered on a building site behind Sloane Square. Pauline befriended them there, bringing them food and affection. When construction began on the site, she decided that something must be done to save the cats. So she rounded them up, had them neutered and brought them down to her house in the country. Around this core of Sloane scavengers has collected a crew of cats from other places, including Strayboy himself, and Tabby who came from a churchyard in Poplar. Another cat was due to arrive from Kilburn on the day after our visit.

During the summer months Pauline takes some of the cats – and

any kittens she has at the sanctuary – up to the Rollright stone circle. This ancient monument of some seventy-seven standing stones (local tradition has it that the number of stones in the circle can never be counted accurately) stands just north of the village of Little Rollright on the Oxfordshire/Warwickshire border. Although administered by English Heritage, the stones are owned and overseen by Pauline. She charges people ten pence to visit the site, putting the modest proceeds towards the running of the cat sanctuary.

The cats are almost as big an attraction as the megaliths, and Pauline has found homes for almost four hundred kittens through visitors to the Rollright stones. She is very scrupulous about ensuring that the kittens will find good homes, often telling visitors to come back the week after if she suspects they are merely choosing a cat on a whim.

Strayboy assists Pauline in administering both the sanctuary and the stones. The other cats recognize and respect his natural authority. He is a cat who once controlled a manor that stretched from Eaton Square to Peter Jones. His tattered ears and grizzled mien tell of a prime spent fighting. Now, however, he has retired from the fray; living in the country, he never hunts or kills anything. He saves his energy to lick the new arrivals into shape, dealing out a brisk cuff to the thoughtless offender or giving a comforting wash-and-brush to an anxious waif.

'He would love to be in charge of the stones too,' says Pauline. Certainly he approves of the changes that she has made at the circle. She has planted a hedge to shield the site from the road and the wind – two of Strayboy's least favourite things – and she has introduced a buddleia bush which attracts butterflies in the summer. Cats are naturally fond of butterflies; they know how fine they look together. They are probably aware that a cat with a butterfly is a Chinese visual pun on the word for happiness; and besides, butterflies are delicious to eat.

Another recent improvement has been the construction of a small, stone caretaker's hut. On a chill summer day it is, in Pauline's and Strayboy's view, much cosier to sit in the hut than out amongst the stones. The floor of the hut is almost completely covered by the enormous old doormat from the Cadogan Hotel – like Pauline and Strayboy, another happy Chelsea transplant. Emblazoned with the name of the hotel (a name forever associated with the arrest of Oscar Wilde), it is a very fine mat, fit to be sat upon by a very fine cat.

# Yoda, Squeak, Minnie the Minx, Catkin,

Red Hall, near Carrickfergus in County Antrim, was obligingly painted red by its nineteenth-century inhabitants. Local antiquarian tradition, however, asserts that the house's origins date back to the medieval Scandinavian period and that its name is derived from a mistranslation of an Old Norse word. The Viking word for an island is very close to the Irish word for red. Popular fancy was happy to conspire in this error. Locals like to suggest that the redness of Red House was supplied by blood shed during a battle in the glen between the followers of the wayward Sorley Boy MacDonnell and the forces of John Chichester, the English governor at Carrickfergus.

The McClintock family have lived at Red Hall since the early years of this century, but the house itself is largely of seventeenth-century construction. It boasts a stunning, Jacobean staircase and two delightful modelled-plaster ceilings. Over the centuries the house had declined into a state of some disrepair – the roof leaked, the plaster sagged, the floorboards creaked. Dampness threatened the rare and beautiful ceilings. But, as disaster loomed, providence smiled. The McClintocks discovered a lost Haydn manuscript in their attic. They auctioned it for a handsome sum and with the proceeds they are restoring the roof.

The centre of McClintock family life is a long way from the roof down in the vast subterranean kitchen, a room that combines the aspect of a mad professor's laboratory with that of an animal refuge. On a large refectory table in the middle of the room stands a rank of five curious-looking flagons filled with home-made wines – oakleaf, peach, rose petal, elderflower and beetroot (an alarming purple colour at this stage, it will, apparently, turn yellow in time). Boxes of papers and bundles of old colour supplements stand in tottering stacks. Under the table two chain saws lie like sleeping pterodactyls amongst the coiled sheaths of extension flex.

Against one yellowing wall stuck with wine labels and lined with dark-wood dressers stand three makeshift dog boxes in which lie three rather makeshift dogs: a large black one, a dotty red setter and an undefined terrier. Along the facing wall runs an impressive Esse stove. At first sight its black enamelled top seemed to sport several impressive kettles, a large Ovaltine tin and little else, but then the blackness began to move and a form stretched itself out of the obscurity and assumed the shape of a cat. My eyes refocused and I began to see that there were four cats – two black and two grey – asleep on the warm stove top. A white-and-tabby cat appeared and

took up a position at the other end.

'We've got eight cats, I think,' Mrs McClintock explained. 'They love the Esse.' The feline roll call is impressive. Squeak is the oldest. A black, neutered male, named because of the piercing squeak he emits when he wants to be let in or out. He is a fastidious gentleman and will only deign to eat food from the McClintocks' own table; dog-food is not to be countenanced.

The other black cat is called Yoda after a character in *Star Wars*. Her great stupidity is balanced by her great soppiness; she loves to be cuddled. Yoda is an enthusiastic foot-fetishist. She cannot resist a bare foot; she will pounce upon it and cover it with scouring licks.

Minnie the Minx, or Minnix as she is known, is perhaps the sharpest cat of the group. A sleek grey female, she has no fear and will chase off undesirable people with a vigour that cannot be denied. 'Minnix has water on the brain,' says Mr McClintock. This turns out to be an intense fascination for the dripping tap by the kitchen sink. Minnix spends a great deal of time and concentrated effort batting with her paw at the falling drops of water.

Minnix, along with Yoda, is the daughter of Blue. Blue is another grey cat, although some of her blood is Siamese, an ancestry testified by her loud and plaintive miaow. Between them these four cats comprise one of the feline power blocks in the McClintock kitchen. They tend to monopolize one end of the Esse, they groom each other, swap anecdotes, and show a haughty disdain towards the dogs and even their own more motley fellows.

Catkin they regard as a bit of an interloper. She was found up a tree but has now taken up a snug position amongst the kettles at the other end of the stove. Catkin, a small, pretty tabby-and-white cat, has an even smaller pretty tabby-and-white kitten called Alder. (The name is both an apt one for another sprig of the willow family and a shortening for Alderman; Alder had a brother with an impressive white collar-marking rather like a chain of office. He was called Mayor.) Alder's ambitions belie his size. His afternoons are spent attacking people sitting on the low wall by the bus-stop at the top of the drive.

Pansy, a black-and-white kitten, the other babe of the moment, is less confident. This is unsurprising, as he was found bedraggled, limping down the road on cracked paws. The McClintocks seem to act as a magnet for unloved and displaced animals. Superannuated donkeys, stray dogs and abandoned kittens all receive a generous welcome at Red Hall.

The tortoiseshell Poppy, if she has not actually abused this welcome, has certainly made the most of it. Poppy is a hypochondriac. As a kitten she made wilful efforts to die on several occasions, and only consented to go on living after a great deal of attention and medicine had been lavished upon her. Even now Poppy refuses to admit that she is quite well. She spends most of

her time curled up on top of a pile of plates in the dark recesses of a kitchen dresser. There she can nurse her ailments in peace.

She does, however, emerge from her retreat at feeding time. Feeding so many animals in a single room requires a degree of planning and strategy. To ease the problem all (with the exception of Squeak) are given tinned dog-food. The three dogs are attached by leads to the stove rail and fed together next to the Esse. The cats eat under the kitchen table next to the chain saws. They share the assortment of plates and dishes with unexpected consideration.

There is a poster above the Esse. It shows a kitten curled happily inside a flowerpot and bears the inscription, 'When you are at peace with yourself any place is home.' While the McClintock cats certainly agree with this proposition they recognize that it is the rare quality of their marvellous home that has given them the blessing of inner peace.

Puss

Puss was not impressed by the prospect of a trip to Wales. Puss is not easily impressed. Alice Thomas Ellis and Puss (along with Alice's large family and son William's cat, Cadmus) live in a large family house in Camden Town. Camden Town may be a very fine setting for many things, but for an interview with an enigmatic cat and a mystical novelist, even Gloucester Crescent seemed to lack quite *l'ambience juste*, the whiff of sacred calm and profane desire.

But Wales had possibilities; a land of druids, saints and stove-pipe hats, of fire-breathing dragons and fire-kindling nationalists. Moreover (and more to the point), Wales is Alice's spiritual home. She was brought up there, she has set novels there, she has a cottage there, she goes there often. And where Alice goes Puss goes.

We all drove down from Camden Town to Wales together, although neither Alice nor Puss drive; not the least of their similarities. Puss, peeved at not having been consulted about arrangements, mewed crossly for a while and then threw up over a rug in the back of the car. We drove on.

Soon the smooth ribbon of the motorway ended and then even the A roads began to shrivel, writhing along the bottom of green valleys, branching at rustic signposts that offered several destinations and no vowels. We were in Powis; Puss was asleep.

Alice Thomas Ellis' Welsh retreat is a charmed settlement of three low, slate cottages under a bristling crag, on whose lower slopes a saintly virgin once dwelt, rescuing hares from impressionable huntsmen and lending *éclat* to the neighbourhood. As we drove up, the afternoon sun enflamed the rash of heather on the mountainside. The lush grass of the valley bottom, browsed by plump sheep, seemed almost to itch with the strutting of dim-wit young pheasants, the lollop of rabbits, perhaps even the headlong streak of a blessed hare. Puss clambered down from the car, picked her way over the lintel, walked slowly up the bare wooden stairs and disappeared under a bed.

Alice Thomas Ellis does not approve of soppy cats, she admires feline independence. 'When they are overly affectionate I think there is something strange,' she admits. 'I like a cat who walks by herself and all places are alike to her. A bit aloof and rather beautiful.' Like Puss.

Alice has always had cats. 'Always, always, always,' except briefly when she had Martha: Martha was a bull-dog. 'Martha was crazy. Poor Martha, we didn't have her long because she was so mad and bit everyone.' One dog was enough. Although a dog may be very

dependable it is also rather dependent. 'A dog is like a man who grows a beard and can't wash his own cricket flannels. They need to be taken for walks,' she says in horror. Small wonder that Alice prefers cats. She has had lots of them over the years, most of them called Puss, although a few started out as Kitty.

The current Puss is small, compact, black as a Welsh bonnet and eight years old. There is a shade of doubt about her origins. 'We've had her since she was tiny,' says Alice. 'I can't think where Puss came from. She must be the kitten of one of our previous cats.'

Puss loves luxury and warmth with the uncomplicated passion of an Eastern princess. 'She is the sort of cat who lies on her divan eating Turkish delight and polishing her nails. She likes sitting under the light or by the Aga; anywhere nice and warm.' But such languorous indolence has to be defended. Other cats are treated with cruel disdain. When Cadmus arrived, large and placid, on the scene and beside the Aga some two years ago, trouble was inevitable.

'We used to think that the trouble was because of Cadders because he was the biggest. There was a lot of *meowrowrow* and chasing around. They broke all the jugs on the shelf chasing each other in the worst early days. I used to say, "That bloody Cadders is so foul, he reminds me of Henry VIII. I hate him, take him away. I'll go and live in a hotel room, or put Cadders in a hotel room." But then we observed them a bit more closely and it wasn't him at all, it was *her* – Puss! Puss would sit there like the good little girl, the one who pulls people's plaits and then those people turn round and swipe them just as the teacher looks up. It was that sort of situation. Puss would sit there, idly minding her own business, and Cadmus would walk past and, wallop – *meowrowrow*. And then Puss would turn round as though it was nothing to do with her. It was a bit mean.' When she was unmasked she was not a bit ashamed. 'I've never seen a cat show guilt. They sometimes look a bit disconcerted, but guilt – never.'

Alice herself is sometimes touched by a twinge of guilt over having had Puss spayed (after she had had two litters). Puss now diverts her considerable maternal instincts and energies towards the sock basket in the laundry. 'I come down in the morning and find socks all over the house. There will be balls of socks littered everywhere. I came down one night and caught Puss at it. She thinks they're kittens! She's carrying them in her mouth, high, with that air of pride and tenderness. It is so touching it makes me cry.' Cadmus, less refined in his tastes, prefers dirty shirts.

The other object of Puss' devotion is the telephone. She has only to hear it ring to appear, silent and intent, beside it. If Alice is engaged in a long conversation Puss will clamber up and sit on the handset, tangle her feet in the cord, and dribble with concentrated contentment. Why? Does the telephone remind Puss of her mother? Certainly the physical resemblance cannot be striking. Puss, however, does have a purr – *purrup purrup* – a bit like the ring of an old telephone, so perhaps she has bakelite in her blood.

Puss tolerates most people with an aloof courtesy, expecting affection and commanding respect. Alice, however, she likes. She will sit on her lap in front of the Aga or curl up beside her on the sofa. Although Puss does not demand (or display) a great deal of demonstrative affection she does expect to have her desires met. 'When she thinks it is time I got up she appears on my bed,

slobbering in my face and scratching gently. That means she wants her breakfast.'

'Cats make their feelings and wants known very, very clearly. They are like the managers of companies who expect to be obeyed. They don't like having to say things twice.'

Puss let us know that she was not particularly interested in being interviewed and photographed but she was prepared to condescend this once. She appeared briefly, but with great presence and Garbo-like self-assurance, at the top of the stairs. And then, having struck some impressive poses, she stalked off to inspect the grounds, scout for mice and confirm her territorial rights. ('Although she's a she, she sprays.' This is either a mark of rather unfeminine aggression or a kidney problem.)

Despite Saint Melangell's concern for persecuted hares, other game in the valley is in open season and Puss supplements her Kit-e-Kat diet with young rabbits and local mice. Due caution, however, must be exercised; a predecessor had his nose nipped painfully by an irate weasel and the local squire is a jealous and armed protector of his inbecile pheasants.

Like her cat, Alice Thomas Ellis' books combine the domestic and reticent with the wild and mysterious, the echo of unexplained laughter. She likes to tell the story of the cat who is sitting at home with his master one night when a great cry rends the air, 'The King of the Cats is dead!' The puss jumps up and shouts, 'Then I am the King of the Cats!' and disappears up the chimney never to be seen again.

Alice also puts cats into her own novels. *The 27th Kingdom* revolves around the enigmatic Focus, a long-haired white cat with a flat foolish face and a penchant for swimming in the sea.

Puss, though less extravagantly eccentric in her habits, is quite as enigmatic. It would not have surprised me if, as we sat watching *The Equalizer* that evening, a cry of 'The Queen of the Cats is dead!' had echoed down the chimney and Puss, galvanized but supremely self-possessed, had answered, 'Then I am the Queen of the Cats!'

# Uncle, Baryshnikov & Tamara Karsavina

Caroline Colthurst describes herself as a 'cat freak'; she is not unworthy of the appellation. She lives in a beautiful old house with three beautiful cats (not to mention a really quite good-looking husband and two striking daughters). These human elements of the family are not mentioned that often, certainly not in comparison to the cats, who dominate the domestic scene with their antics and demands.

The Colthursts and their cats live at Pitchford Hall, near Shrewsbury. It is one of the most handsome buildings in England. A large, E-plan, brown-and-white, half-timbered house, it was built towards the end of the sixteenth century by Mr Ottley, a wealthy Shropshire merchant. It has never been sold since. For over four hundred years it has been passed on within the family, gathering an interesting collection of furniture and a distinctive aura of gracious domesticity, rare in a house so grand and old.

The house is full of cats. Many of these, however, are made of papier mâché, and others adorn the walls (Mrs Colthurst has several original pictures of Orlando the Marmalade Cat), but three of the cats are very real indeed.

Caroline's three real cats are called Uncle, Baryshnikov and Tamara Karsavina. Uncle's proper name is Runtlestiltskin (he was the runt of his litter) but this became familiarized to Uncle Runtle and has now been pared down to plain Uncle. He is a seal-pointed Siamese, with fine features and delicate sensibilities. 'He has terrible "feelings" and a great tendency towards taking umbrage,' explains Caroline. 'He is neutered and a complete idiot. But we love him dearly.'

The great adventure in Uncle's life was when he was kitnapped. He disappeared for several weeks (previously he had not so much as spent a night out) and after extensive searches he was given up for dead. Baryshnikov was bought, a tearful purchase to replace poor Uncle and provide company for the now-dead Chocolata. But no sooner was Baryshnikov installed than Uncle reappeared. He was dumped unceremoniously back in the driveway. The kitnappers had not counted upon his 'terrible feelings' and had been unable to cope with a cat of such a nice disposition. They were obliged to admit defeat. Uncle survived the ordeal unscathed. He had always supposed that the world was full of petty injustices and vexations, largely focused upon his unfortunate self. To be kidnapped and then returned as unacceptable seemed only to confirm him in his prejudices.

In his heyday, Baryshnikov (known as Nishko) could boast an impressive bag. One brisk spell saw him carry off over forty-five grey squirrels, five stoats, a fully-grown cock pheasant (out of season), a wild mallard, a rat or two, and untold numbers of mice, voles and shrews. Now the pace has slowed somewhat. Age has curbed his speed and perhaps his appetite for the chase, and a family of owls has taken up residence in the half-timbered seventeenth-century tree-house in the garden, competing with Nishko for the first bite of the smaller rodents.

Despite his fierceness in the field, Nishko has a nature as soft and pliable as his elegant form. A lithe brown Burmese, with seductively lazy olive-green eyes, he happily abandons himself to the pleasures of a comfy chair, a welcoming lap or a sun-soaked patch of carpet. When he was younger the daughters of the house would dress him up in doll's clothes and parade him about in a toy pram. Nishko loved it. He is a very floppy cat, delighted to be rolled onto his back and tickled, or wrapped across Mrs Colthurst's shoulders. Nor is he jealous of his affections; he greets all visitors with a welcoming mien, graciously offering his back to be stroked and his head to be rubbed. He will even see you to bed. 'He is a complete whore,' laments Caroline.

Tamara Karsavina (Mrs Naughty to you, me and everybody else) has experienced the smooth as well as the rough. A properly supervised liaison with a Burmese stud produced eight delightful Tonkanese kittens. Now, however, she is in the thrall of 'a hideous, earless, manky, farm tom cat. We call him Moriarty but I think his name may be Toby.' She is a prolific and excellent mother. When we visited she was just getting over having had a litter of eight kittens. All but one had departed. Little Lucifer, a grey and white dynamo, was still in residence, awaiting the arrival of the new caretaking couple who had been promised a kitten to show them the ropes in their new surroundings. Lucifer was busy living up to his devilish name.

Mrs Naughty, kind and generous though she is, is not untouched by diabolical mystery herself. Her mother was a witch's cat from across the Welsh border. There is some speculation that Mrs Naughty might be an incupuss. She is certainly more intelligent than her 'brothers', and is given to displays of surprising fierceness if her kittens are threatened; but her behaviour in the main suggests that she is touched by white, rather than black, magic.

All three cats are alive to the supernatural echoes that

reverberate around the ancient walls of Pitchford Hall. A visiting
fortune-teller (perhaps a disciple of Russell Grant) remarked,
'Ghosts? My dear, the place is absolutely stuffed with them.' The
suddenly-encountered aroma of cigar smoke, a vestige of Caroline's
dead step-father, has been experienced by over eighty guests. But
other apparitions, although less common, are no less real: the little
old lady in the upper corridor, the man in green armour, the stout
fellow in the library. While these spectres appear only sometimes to
human eyes, the cats can be seen tracking the movement of
invisible figures, with keen, unwavering gaze.

Mrs Colthurst has only three cats because she would be unable to fit any more on to her lap. Inevitably there is a degree of friction among the cats about who sits where, but such disputes are brief and mild. Uncle adores Nishko, doubtless awed by his prowess in the hunt, and Nishko is content to return the affection, although occasionally some unthinking act of stupidity on Uncle's part prompts a swift cuff from the amiable Burmese bully.

Uncle, aware of her intelligence, is studiously polite to Mrs Naughty. Nishko, however, resents her. And both boys go into a terrible sulk when Mrs Naughty has kittens, as the little ones become the centre of attention, and their mother becomes snappish and sharp.

All three cats will, however, act in concert if threatened. A visitor's Jack Russell had to be rescued and carried to the safety of the car by its startled owner after it had been cornered by the three cats, operating together with menacing intent. The Colthursts' own dogs have long since learnt to treat the cats with the respect that they demand. They have come to accept the cats' insistence on accompanying them and Caroline on their morning walk. The sight of this merry but unlikely caravan alarms the cows and starts the horses. The farmer stalled his tractor when he first encountered them in the lane.

Like the dogs, Mr Colthurst has learnt to live with the cats. Caroline recalls that, 'The first question I asked Oliver on our first outing was, "Do you like cats?" To which he replied, "My mother loved them." Sometimes he pretends to be aloof, but after twenty years of marriage he fundamentally likes them. He has to. Poor man, he often has to share his bed with the three of them and me. Two of Mrs Naughty's litters were actually born on our bed with us there too.'

This ability to surprise and amaze is just one of the many things that attracts Caroline to cats. The springs of her affection for them are many. She relishes their elegant contours and the tactile pleasures of their fur. On account of this she prefers short-haired cats to their long-haired cousins. They are smoother if not softer. But most of all Caroline loves the company of her cats. 'They're fun. They can be very loving, or in a terrible huff. And they do have the amazing capacity to mop up all one's emotions, whether happy or sad, leaving one calmer and feeling better. Also, they're wonderful hot-water bottles; they don't get cold in the night.' They probably say the same about her.

# Tigers

'God made the cat in order that man might have the pleasure of caressing the tiger,' wrote the French poet Ferdinand Mery. Whatever the truth of the statement, it is one that Terry Whittaker can afford to ignore; it does not apply to him. He has the pleasure of stroking tigers every day. Terry is the head cat-keeper at John Aspinall's Port Lympne zoo park.

Amongst his feline charges he has five Siberian tigers and eight Indian ones, including two young cubs which he and his wife, Jackie, are raising at home by hand. When we visited them the two cubs were only three weeks old. They are called Pindi and Thana. At three weeks a tiger is the size of a puppy dog; its eyes are open and beginning to focus but their colour has not yet changed from violet-blue to hazel. The rest of the fabled tiger colouring, however, is there – the distinctive black stripes, the white ruff, the fearful symmetry of the patterned mask and the spots on the backs of the ears. Some of these features stand out of proportion; the graceful lineaments of the adult tiger are only hinted at in the outsize head, the shovel paws and the thin, pointed tail of the young animal.

Thana and Pindi live, along with a blue teddybear, in a little pen in the Whittakers' back room. They are fed – a little every three hours – on powdered milk. They will continue to live in the house until they are three or four months old, although they will gradually be introduced to a caged enclosure in the garden.

At present they spend their days staggering with ungainly grace across the floors of the Whittakers' home. They stumble into and over each other, and even trip over their own feet. Their front paws, upon whose size and strength they would depend in the wild, are like boxing gloves at the end of their little front legs. The paws are set at a slightly splayed angle and, occasionally, they move off in different directions, tipping the tottering cub down onto its nose.

Such a tumble – and, indeed, almost every other event and sensation – is greeted with a squeak of pleasure or protest. Tiger cubs are very vocal animals. They maintain a near-constant barrage of little mews and shrieks during their waking hours. Like the more reticent adult, they greet welcome visitors with a noisy exhalation which sounds somewhat like 'fffurraawawawwa', the tigerish equivalent of 'How do you do' and is well worth mastering, lest one should ever encounter a forward tiger on one's travels.

Despite their tender years, or weeks, the two cubs are already beginning to reveal their distinctive personalities. Pindi, the smaller of the pair, is the sharper. She is galvanized by a ceaseless and questing curiosity. Thana prefers comfort and quiet, a warm room and a lap to doze upon. 'Pindi looks like her mother,' says Jackie. 'She will be very pretty.'

Certainly Pindi and Thana's mother is very pretty. She is called Khala. She shares an enclosure with the twins' father, Nari, and her two elder children. Khala was given every chance to nurse her two new cubs but, as Terry puts it, 'she just couldn't cope.' So, reluctantly, it was decided to raise them by hand.

As the cubs are a pair they can, for much of the time, amuse and comfort each other. They sleep together in a tangle of black and orange, creating strange patterns with their markings. When they wake, they sometimes suckle on each other's ears for comfort or wrestle together in boisterous play. 'They need each other a lot,' says Jackie.

'Even grown tigers like each other's company,' says Terry. 'But, like the domestic cat, they're also very independent. In the wild they always hunt on their own.' Perhaps more important for humans working with tigers, they are extremely direct animals. 'Tigers are very honest creatures; very frank about what they want and what they are going to do.' Terry regularly enters the enclosures of the adults, greeting them with a playful slap and the distinctive 'ffurraawawawwa' snort, as well as such choice human endearments as 'Hello rat-bag'. He is very alive to their moods and feelings. If they are vexed by his presence he is quick to notice it and as quick to leave their enclosure.

Although the tiger cubs are frank in their demands for food and attention, they are also respectful of authority; they respond well to discipline. 'They're not like the Barbary lion cub we once reared,' recalls Jackie. 'If you slapped her, she would slap you right back!'

Tigers have too much natural dignity to behave in such a wayward fashion. Although older tiger cubs will take a playful swipe at passing legs, they never become as obstreperous as some other big-cat offspring. Tigers never forget that they are monarchs of the jungle.

Amazing though it seems, not everyone is impressed by their regal airs. Until recently the Whittakers had a cat called Timothy. (He died last year.) Throughout his life he endured the intrusion into his home of numerous lion and tiger cubs. 'Timothy sorted out all the big cats who ever came to stay,' says Terry. 'He was completely undaunted by them.' Timothy believed that a cat can not only look at a king, he can also box him on the nose.

# Possum & Brindle

'I'm not an animal lover,' says Faith Raven. 'My children sometimes complain that I ruined their lives by not allowing them to keep dogs. I knew that I would be left with the dogs while they were off having fun. But now, having had five children and a husband who've all disappeared in different directions, I find the cats are very good company.'

Mrs Raven has two cats, Possum and Brindle. She got two so that they could not only keep her company but also each other – when she was off having fun. They are both neutered males but they are not related. Possum comes from the local egg-lady near Mrs Raven's Queen Anne manor house in Cambridgeshire, while Brindle is a Scottish cat from the village near the Ravens' house in Argyll. They are both five years old.

Possum is the larger of the pair. His coat is an attractive design of white with orange patches; his face is white and expressive, enlivened by hawk-tipped ears. He is very proud of his well-turned limbs, and loses no opportunity to loll about, ostentatiously stretching his legs to show off their handsome proportions.

Brindle by contrast is smaller and neater. He is, true to his name, brindled: a long-haired, brown-and-black tabby with an elegant white bodice and a rather less elegant white smudge on his face. While Possum was chosen to set off Faith's hair colour, Brindle was selected because he reminded her of a much-loved former cat.

When the family first moved to their house in the village of Shepreth they were adopted by a partially wild cat who lived in one of the farm buildings at the end of the garden. 'She was stripey,' Faith recalls, 'so we called her Stripey; so original.' Andrew, the eldest son, however, who was very young at the time, insisted on calling the cat Ripey. Ripey had kittens, all of which were disposed of save one which the Ravens adopted and called, with scarcely more originality, Thomas. Thomas was a fixture of family life, accepted without question. 'But he became ill, so we started to love him. He wheezed a great deal, like my husband, John; they were invalids together. I was into social work at the time and I believed that the cat should be allowed to die naturally.' He did. Then four years ago, when Mrs Raven went to chose a kitten as a companion for Possum, she was struck by Brindle's resemblance to Thomas and selected him in memory of the (naturally) late Tom.

In many ways the characters of Brindle and Possum are as complementary as their looks. The verdict of Mrs Root, the sprightly nonagenarian who used to help Mrs Raven's mother and a friend of the family (and of the cats), is that Possum 'comes walking back into the house just for his meals, swaggers about and goes off again – just like a man.' Brindle is 'like a little girl,' or, at best, somewhere between a man and a little girl. Certainly Possum seems to enjoy masculine company. When there are workmen in the house or gardeners around the kitchen table, Possum is to be found, happy, in their midst. Brindle, however, prefers the caresses of women. 'He sucks up to me dreadfully,' says Faith.

Although Possum is a voracious eater, Brindle is the expert mouser. 'He always has mice for breakfast,' says Faith with mild distaste. 'He plays with them in a rather unattractive way and then eats them in the room next to my bedroom; there are bloodstains on the carpet.'

When in Cambridgeshire, Possum feels himself to be on home territory and spends such time as he is not sleeping and eating wandering about the village. He is a frequent and popular visitor at the pub. When he was still quite young, he disappeared for a fortnight. He had almost been despaired of when, by pure but happy chance, he was recognized sitting in a cage at a nearby cat-sanctuary by the daily's daughter. He was duly reclaimed, but the sanctuary now regard Possum as an alumnus and send round 'a sort of probation officer' to check on him. The ordeal has done nothing to curb his venturesomeness.

When, however, Faith and the cats remove to Scotland for the summer Possum seldom steps out of doors while Brindle, who at Shepreth confines himself to the garden, wanders freely over the estate, the tang of the Highland air and the salty breeze mingling in his appreciative nostrils. He is at home in the heather.

When Brindle was very ill, racked with a 'churchyard cough', Faith brought him to Ardtornish and nursed him back to health with Scottish air and antibiotics. The drugs, sent from the vet on the Isle of Mull, were delivered with Compton MacKenzie-ish drama by the passing ferryboat. The recuperative properties of the Argyll air are not to be underestimated. When Possum nearly had his tail bitten off in a fight and the Cambridge vet counselled amputation, Mrs Raven whisked the battered cat up to Scotland where he effected a full and miraculous recovery.

Different though their characters and origins may be, the two cats do get on well. 'They play tremendously,' says Faith, 'although sometimes they get out of hand and start scratching like two old eunuchs – not that I know what an old eunuch is like; at least I

don't think I know any eunuchs – but you can never be sure.'
Possum used to be the dominant cat, but now the relationship has
changed and Brindle plays the role of the naughty brother,
demanding attention and provoking reactions from the stately
Possum.

Although they rarely sit together in the same room, they
alternate their positions, taking turns in favoured chairs and nooks.
They keep each other company when Mrs Raven is away. Brindle,
who has Siamese blood in his viens, has taught the previously silent
Possum how to talk. They are further united by a common passion
for venison. They lay siege to the larder if they suspect that there is
a morsel of venison in the offing. Few can resist their imploring
looks and their obvious pleasure in a titbit.

Mrs Raven takes obvious pleasure in her two cats. 'They are very
amusing to watch,' she says. She admires their curiosity and their
directness. 'They love one opening doors for them.' Possum has
even learnt to open doors for himself. He greatly alarmed the
gardener by slowly turning the bathroom doorhandle as he,
thinking the house was empty, lay soaking in the tub.

Both cats are great admirers of the gardener's efforts. Mrs Raven
and her late husband have created and nurtured beautiful gardens
both in Cambridgeshire and Scotland; the cats appreciate this.
'They like to go out in the morning, like gentlemen going to the
club.' And in the evening one of the cats will accompany Faith
around the garden, showing off for her benefit and amusement,
climbing trees, scratching the bark, and behaving like an excitable
dog.

Inside the house they are calmer. 'I've never seen them break
anything. They even sharpen their claws without pulling out the
threads from the upholstery.' Nevertheless they do like attention.
'They love to be made a fuss of,' admits Faith. 'People say that cats
are selfish, but really they are egocentric, not selfish.' Although
Faith respects their egocentricity and even loves them for it, she
does recognize that there are limits.

When we arrived, one of the cats had that morning been sick all
over Faith's bed. 'An awful experience,' she said. After months of
talking to cat-lovers I mumbled something to the effect that I was
sure the poor cat would get over it. 'What do you mean the poor
cat?' asked Faith. 'It was an awful experience for me. It was my bed.'

# Tiger

'When he was small he looked a bit like a tiger, but we soon found out he was not like a tiger at all.' Tiger shows no trace of shame at not living up to his forceful name. He sits happily by the fire and smiles to himself. Tiger is Tom Kime's cat. He is a large, long-haired, black-and-brown tabby with a huge white ruff, and a passion for lounging about doing not very much. Tiger is about five years old, Tom is about thirteen.

Tiger and his sister Poppy live with Tom and his sister Hannah (and Hannah's and Tom's parents, Robert and Helen Kime) in a beautiful eighteenth-century house near Marlborough. Helen (as Helen Nicoll) is the author of the bestselling *Meg and Mog* books, but Tiger is certainly not the model for Mog, the witch's cat; he is much happier on a sofa than on a broomstick. At Dene House he has the choice of several fine and handsome perches as Robert is an antique dealer and the house is rich with the proofs of his acumen and taste. But abundance can be confusing and, with so many inviting pieces of furniture to choose between, Tiger often gives up and lies on the floor in front of the Aga. The flagstones there are warm and, moreover, provide a fine, matt background for his coat of many colours.

The active, predatory existence of his larger, Indian namesake does not appeal to Tiger. While not a paid-up member of the anti-bloodsport lobby, he has little inclination or aptitude for the chase. 'Sometimes he catches a mouse,' says Tom. 'Sometimes.' For the most part, however, he sleeps and eats.

Although he is not prepared to catch his food he is happy to scavenge for it. The effort is less taxing and the prize both more certain and more valuable. He frequently jumps into the dustbins in search of discarded titbits and once he feasted upon the still-palpitating innards of a trout which Tom had caught and was gutting in the garden.

Tiger loves the garden – and well he might; it is very lovely. While most people admire the luxuriant planting from above, Tiger delights in enjoying it from below. During the summer he spends such sunny days as there are, lolling beneath the shading fronds of the shrubs and flowers. He is also particularly fond of a pillar-like yew tree near the back door. He disappears into its dense greenness, climbs up inside and then peeps out from amongst the needles.

He has other favoured spots for observing the comings and goings at the back door. Either balanced neatly on one of the broad upright supports of the fruit cage or lying on the sun-warmed panes of the

glasshouse roof, Tiger can survey his domain in comfort and safety.

While Tiger is always happy to *survey* his domain, he is not very proficient at defending it from intruders. A magnetically-operated cat-flap was recently installed in an effort to prevent an unruly local tom from walking in and eating Tiger's supper. Tiger himself had been unable to see off the interloper and had left the task to Tom. Operating the new-fangled cat-flap is, however, also beyond the range of Tiger's accomplishments. He now has to be let in and out on demand.

One of Tiger's ploys for gaining attention is his dramatic impersonation of a carpet bar. He lies, out of sight, on the bottom step of the stairs. As someone descends, he waits until the last moment before springing up and running off. It is an effective attention-grabber, not least because such skittish behaviour is so uncharacteristic of Tiger.

He does still have occasional kittenish romps with his sister Poppy, but such exertions are rare. For the most part brother and sister move along separate paths, courteous yet distant.

In a house full of beautiful things Tiger is unabashedly confident that he is not the least among them. Nevertheless he does show a great deal of respect for the many fine objects that crowd the shelves and tables of his home. 'He never knocks things over,' says Helen. He can pick his way across the dresser, through a mine-field of glass and crockery without incident. 'He has,' as Helen puts it, 'natural grace.'

Tom's reasons for liking cats are not confined to their 'natural grace'. 'They're not smelly – like some dogs,' he says with much truth. 'They're small and neat. You can pick them up and love them. And they're very independent; they don't need to be let in and out.' Unless, of course, they can't operate the magnetic cat-flap.

Although Tiger is not the most independent and adventurous of felines, his predecessor, Tic Toc, was prodigious in this respect. Tic Toc used to follow Tom into the village on visits to the shops. And he would accompany Helen and Robert if they were walking out to dinner nearby, sitting outside and waiting for them so that he could see them safely home afterwards. Sadly he was less conscientious about his own safety. He used up his nine lives in a series of wild adventures. One of them involved him being carried off on the roof of a visiting motorcar and thrown into the hedge on the verge of the A4 several miles down the road.

His most spectacular ordeal, however, was when he stowed away in the back of an antiques delivery van and was driven all the way up to Birmingham. When the delivery men opened the back of the van Tic Toc shot out through the door in a state of extreme agitation and ran forty feet up a tree. Eventually he was coaxed down and arrangements were made for his safe return to Wiltshire. Tom, who had been almost as distraught as Tic Toc, stood by to

receive his poor cat, ready to comfort and soothe the distressed pet. The van drew up and Tic Toc was discovered, not mewing piteously, but curled contentedly on the driver's lap. The cat, pleased to be home, leapt down lightly and, far from demanding comfort and succour of his master, rolled happily in the earth of the vegetable patch.

Tiger seems mightily unimpressed by these tales of Tic Toc's travels. Inertia is his guiding principle. His manner suggests that he does not need to travel in search of exotic pleasures, nor does he have to witness the horrors of Birmingham, to appreciate the fragrant earth of his own vegetable patch. He has the rare gift of contentment.

# *Jambo*

It is a brave man who theorizes about cats. All cat-lovers know that the principal feline trait is contrariness; you can only rely on a cat to be unreliable. But Desmond Morris is a brave man. Having devoted much of his life to studying human behaviour, he has moved on from the open fields of *Manwatching* to the deep arcana of the cat world. His two books, *Catwatching* and *Catlore*, are international bestsellers. They were inspired by Jambo.

Jambo is the large black cat that shares Desmond Morris' studio-cum-library in Oxford. Although Jambo is a black cat she is not completely black, having a small white patch on her front and three white whiskers. Desmond has a theory that nearly all 'black' moggs have a touch of white about them, pure black cats having been persecuted out of existence during the Middle Ages when they were regarded as the devil's familiars.

Jambo arrived up an appletree in Desmond's Oxford garden over ten years ago. She was yowling piteously. Desmond and his family had just returned from safari in Kenya. They were in feline mood, having spent the weeks before amongst lions and cheetahs, and here was a roaring cat up their own appletree.

Desmond hailed it with the traditional Swahili greeting, 'Jambo', and then, urged by his eight-year-old son, he climbed up the tree to rescue the cat. As the erstwhile Curator of Mammals at London Zoo, Desmond was used to handling nervous animals but, perched precariously on a ladder, he was unprepared for this cat's alarm. 'She was terrified,' he recalls. 'I got badly scratched. Somebody had done something awful to this cat. It was terrified of being picked up.'

Desmond managed to bring the cat down and gave her a saucer of milk. She lapped it up hungrily. Jambo decided to stay. At first she lived in the Morrises' home, a large North Oxford brick house, the former residence of James Murray, first editor of the *Oxford English Dictionary*. But when Desmond's wife, Ramona, got some dogs, Jambo moved into Desmond's library, a converted coach-house connected to the main house by a covered passage. The library boasts about 6,600 volumes, including a hundred dictionaries (an apt collection for the owner of Murray's house) and a case of Morris' own numerous publications in their still more numerous editions. The shelves and tables are crowded with handsome books, pre-Columbian pots and African statuettes. Jambo has found herself in congenial surroundings.

Although she retains her horror of being picked up, Jambo has become very friendly towards Desmond over the years. Each morning, when she returns from her inspection of the estate, she engages in an elaborate greeting ritual, rubbing up against his legs and purring loudly. Both of them obviously enjoy the ceremony. 'I sometimes think it is the only reason she goes out,' says Desmond.

With the patience of a zoologist and the enthusiasm of a cat-lover, Desmond has worked hard to establish a rapport with Jambo. 'When you are alone with your cat you do behave in a ridiculous way, a way no grown-up should be seen to behave. I lie on the carpet and try to talk to Jambo in cat-ese (or is it cat-ish?). Occasionally we get a reaction going.'

But even these intimate chats have failed to dispel the memory of the mysterious horror of Jambo's early life. Desmond expounded eloquently on the quasi-Freudian effect of Jambo's trauma. An unfortunate act of human cruelty in early kittenhood had polluted Jambo's attitude towards physical contact forever, rendering her 'thigmophobic', an impressive testament to feline memory and, alas, human cruelty.

This being the case, Desmond had suggested that a photograph of himself holding the cat would be a near impossibility. Toby would have to stand ready, camera primed, finger hovering above the motor-drive button. On previous occasions photographers had had rather less than three seconds to take their pictures before Jambo, uttering a strange primordial wail, would twist from Desmond's grasp and disappear from the room, her tail wagging furiously. Was it worth Toby coming at all?

A cat photographer, however, is schooled in adversity and not easily dismayed. Anxious, but not without hope, Toby set up his tripod and adjusted his camera. His eye to the viewfinder, his finger on the shutter-release, he gave Desmond the 'all clear'. Desmond swooped down lightly on the sleeping Jambo and picked her up. Toby fired off some brisk shots. Desmond nervously awaited the outburst of feline displeasure. Jambo stared calmly at the camera. The shutter continued to click-click furiously. Perspiration glistened on Desmond's brow. The three seconds extended themselves slowly towards thirty. As the film ran out and Desmond's arms started to ache, Jambo uttered a low yet plaintive mew and asked to be set down. Desmond obliged and Jambo padded off to sit under the television set, unmindful of our amazement. It was a rare and happy instance of feline contrariness redounding to our advantage. (Sadly, the photographs were unusable; in his excitement, Toby had forgotten to take off the lens cap.)

Jambo's domestic indolence is balanced by a keen hunting instinct. On her adventures she has lost two of her nine lives in snares on the nearby allotments. On both occasions she has been rescued and returned. The first time, Jambo, having been discovered in the trap, was taken to a local vet who, impressively, treated her at once before advertising her description on the local radio. By chance Desmond heard the announcement and was able to recover Jambo (and pay the vet).

Such incidents have led Jambo to reduce the scope of her patrols. She does, however, still defend her territory with great energy, transforming herself into 'a spitting fury' as she sees off other cats. Desmond is even anxious for the safety of an urban fox which sometimes appears on the studio roof.

Jambo poses a threat not only to the local wildlife but also to Desmond's collection of ethnic artefacts. She has already sent one large pre-Columbian pot crashing to the floor. It is uncertain whether this was due to carelessness or a desire for attention.

Certainly Jambo likes attention, especially when Desmond is at his desk. 'She breaks into my concentration a bit, but that's good. She acts as a punctuation point, a minor and controllable distraction that breaks up the process and makes writing less solitary.'

While Jambo can be a distraction, she can also act as an inspiration. She provided the idea and much of the material for the two cat books. Nor is Desmond inspired only to *write* about cats; as a painter he is a great admirer of the feline form. 'A cat's grace is enormously appealing,' he says. 'It is almost impossible for a cat to get into an ugly position.' In the late 1940s Desmond produced a series of surrealist monotypes based on some of the strange postures taken up by his cat Brinley.

Jambo is unimpressed by these paper rivals. Sitting square and content beneath the television, she devotes herself to the fascinating activity of Morriswatching.

# Angelica

While some cats are content to sit by the hearth, confining their horizons to the fire and the food bowl, and their accomplishments to purring and preening, others seek the riches of variety, the thrill of action and the will to power. Angelica is such a cat.

Angelica belongs to Raffaella Barker and lives at her parents' house in Norfolk. Bintry House, the Barker home, is a pretty flint-faced cottage surrounded by trees. Its sloping walls and tilting ceilings are supported by ancient beams and, in the play-room, by a tree branch wedged between the mantelpiece and the sagging plaster. The house is full of animals (and Barkers).

Besides two dogs – a large mongrel called T-shirt in tribute to his eccentric colouring and a honey-coloured Labrador – there are five cats. True Grit, the lusty tom, is rarely in residence. His amorous exploits take him out of the house a lot. He cadges food off several families in the village, posing as an unfortunate but friendly stray much in need of a bite to eat and a kind word.

Desdemona and Witten, on the other hand, seldom leave the confines of Bintry House. They are refugees from the world; it is too cruel and complicated for them. Desdemona is pretty but hopeless. Her attempts to steal food from the table often result in her dragging the plate down on top of her own head. Whilst she reels, drenched in gravy and stunned by the blow, the dogs eat the loot. Such humiliations have taken their toll and, as an outward sign of an inner hopelessness, Desdemona's tail, once a luxuriant plume, has withered to a fatigued bottle-brush. Witten too is not the handsome cat he once was. As his expectations have sunk so have his ears. They are now flat against his head. Witten spends his days curled up on a shelf, happy but asleep.

Bintry House is, however, far from being a home for distressed gentle cats. The newest feline arrival is Boris who belongs to Raffaella's younger sister, Lily. Though gentle, Boris is anything but distressed. He is a very bold black kitten; fearless, inquisitive and adorable. He trips about the house and garden, a blur of black fluff, his bright eyes, pale as apricots and round as tiddlywinks, turning upon each new thing with undisguised interest and intelligence.

And then there is Angelica. Angelica is a golden cat, with golden fur and golden eyes and a golden mind, a cat that hunts and flies and swims, that drinks white rum and runs the house. Angelica is three years old but wears an air of wisdom and assurance that belies her tender age. She is variously described as being 'like Hitler', 'like a wayward duchess' and 'like one of those dreadful French women who knows the best cuts of meat to buy.' And yet, for all this, she is loved by most and admired by all.

Raffaella was given Angelica by a local friend as a companion for her when she first left home. Raffaella duly treated the cat as a friend, including it in her plans, sharing her food with it, asking it questions and telling it stories. Angelica, grateful for some intelligent conversation, took to speaking back, chirruping sprightly answers to Raffaella's questions.

Nor was this the only sign of Angelica's intelligence. She developed a hatred of Raffaella's motorcar because she knew that it always led to the vet. 'I used to take her to the vet a great deal,' Raffaella explains. 'The vet is one of the very few things you can spend money on in Norfolk.'

When Raffaella came to live in London she could not bear the prospect of Angelica's misery on the long drive up to town so she dosed her (and Witten who was coming too) with special cat tranquillizers. The medication was a success and the cats dozed quietly on the trip down the motorway. Unfortunately, once in London, Raffaella was held up in heavy traffic and the cats regained consciousness, springing back to life, crazed and dazed, just as she was negotiating Hyde Park Corner. As she edged into the flow of traffic, Angelica and Witten leapt about the car, pressing their faces to the windows and wailing at the passing traffic. It was not a good introduction to London life for any of them.

Raffaella recovered her composure more quickly than the cats. But then, she was able to go out and about. The cats were not. Angelica and Witten hated London. To be stuck in a flat with a litter-tray for company was no sort of life compared to frolicking under the broad pale skies of north Norfolk. Witten's ears began their decline. Angelica took more direct action and protested vigorously. Raffaella could not but be swayed by such an eloquent appeal (and by the distressing sight of Witten's lugs). Angelica and Witten returned to Norfolk on the train. They travelled in a cardboard box and alarmed fellow passengers by sticking their heads through the cardboard and yowling.

Safely ensconced at Bintry House, Witten continued his slow decline. Angelica, however, set about taking control of the place. No one was, or is, allowed to ignore her. She loves nothing more than destroying the Sunday papers, even as they are being read. First she sits on the open newspaper, covering the print and demanding to be stroked. Then, suspecting that you might be trying to read round her, she rolls about on the page. Reading is now impossible but Angelica, concerned to display her power and her disrespect for newspaper journalism, will then claw the paper to shreds.

Angelica has long been aware of the dramatic power of destruction. 'She is an appalling show-off,' admits Raffaella. 'She will knock over vases and sit on cakes just to get attention.' Angelica does, however, have subtler charms. 'She is a mistress of the extended limb,' explains Raffaella's mother, Elspeth. By striking elegant poses she convinces everyone of her beauty. Moreover, while lounging decorously upon some well-appointed surface she can stretch out a paw to swipe a passing cat or dog, or prod a negligent human who is daring to ignore her and, maybe, bestowing attention upon some unworthy rival such as Desdemona or T-shirt.

It is a brave man who refuses to give Angelica the respect and attention she feels she deserves. One day Raffaella's father, George, was preparing himself a lunchtime treat of some smoked salmon. Leaving it on the kitchen table for an instant as he fetched some butter from the fridge, he turned just in time to see Angelica starting into his lunch. George, moving with the speed and fury of an enraged poet, cuffed Angelica from the table, uttering a fearful oath. Angelica, matching fury with fury, fixed George with a cold, cold glare and stalked from the room.

Early the next morning, as George lay in bed enjoying his matutinal cuppa, Angelica opened the door and walked in. Ignoring Elspeth, whom she normally greets, Angelica leapt up on to the bed and strode on to George's lap. George, a cup of tea in one hand a biscuit in the other, was powerless to resist as Angelica, with deliberate slowness, turned around, spread her haunches and, with unerring aim, pissed on his chest. Writhing in horror George managed to shake Angelica from the bed. She then pissed on his trousers where they lay on the floor. George, not a noted cat-lover, is now one of Angelica's most fervent admirers.

Although Angelica thrives upon admiration and is not beyond showing affection herself, she is never soppy. Even when she is being stroked her loud purr sounds like a well-geared engine, its rhythm always suggesting that you, the stroker, could do better. While Angelica agrees to accompany Elspeth on her walks, 'she thinks it very vulgar to follow anyone, so she saunters along pretending she has nothing to do with you, or leaps and bounds from cover to cover, stalking you rather than walking with you.'

It is all good practice, for Angelica is a mighty hunter. Some of her predatory zeal and ingenuity is focused on the domestic front. Angelica's expressive limbs are not only used to direct attention towards herself; she also uses her dexterity to open doors, particularly fridge doors. The fridge at Bintry is barricaded with chairs, but I fear that the measure merely serves to alert Angelica to the excitements that lie within. Moreover it increases the challenge – and therefore the pleasure – of a successful raid. 'Angelica knows which day the butcher comes and she lies in wait,' laments Elspeth.

Angelica lies in wait for a great deal more than just the butcher's

van. The chronicle of her slaying would shame some of the gorier pages of the *Iliad*. Mice, rabbits, shrews, voles, pheasants, partridges, weasels and ducks fill the columns of her game book. She also chases more exotic prey. Down at the water's edge she stalks the hideous coypu, a cross between a beaver and a rat, imported for its fur but now roaming free along the riverbanks of East Anglia. The coypu is the size of a small dog, with black fur and large orange teeth. The government employs a man to catch them. Armed with lethal snares and ingenious traps he manages to cull about three a year. Angelica can kill that many in a week.

Unlike most cats Angelica is not afraid of water. Indeed she relishes it. She lurks in the reed beds, preying upon unsuspecting ducklings. In the summer she even plucks trout out of the stream. Not content, however, with holding sway over the earth and the waters, Angelica is set on extending her hegemony to include the air. She perches upon the ledge of an upper-storey window, watching the housemartins wheel and swoop. Then, fixing her eye upon a particularly tender-looking morsel, she launches herself, an orange missile, into the air, plucking the flying bird from the sky and landing nimbly with it dead in her jaws. Diana would be proud of her.

The chaste goddess might be less impressed with Angelica's fecundity. Her predatory prowess is tempered by a highly developed maternal instinct. Sometimes, of course, these two strands cross; she brings Boris freshly-slaughtered prey to give him the scent of the hunt. She lavishes attention on her own kittens, who are nearly always beautiful and nearly always go on to rule over the households that adopt them. She also looks after Desdemona's litters as Desdemona is wholly unable to cope with the demands of motherhood.

Angelica is always faithful to True Grit, not because he is a considerate lover, an attentive husband or a concerned father but because his battered good looks combine happily with her own mysterious elegance to create beautiful kittens. Vanity is all.

It has long been a puzzle where Angelica gets her mysterious elegance from. Though Norfolk born and bred, her golden eyes hint at some illustrious and mythical past. Some light was cast upon the matter when George was in Luxor last February. Sitting upon the pleasantly-shaded terrace, sipping a mint julep, he felt something brush against his leg. Glancing down he saw a golden kitten, the image of Angelica, the same expression of imperious command blazing in its eyes.

Surely Egypt is Angelica's ancestral home. She never forgets, and she allows no one else to forget, that her forebears were worshipped by nations and dandled upon the laps of Pharaohs, that the blood of Bastet, the cat goddess, still flows in her veins.

# Wilberforce

In the political life of all nations and every epoch there are unheralded figures, hidden yet influential: shadowy presences who have affected the outcome of important events, set the tone of whole administrations, counselled the powerful and protected the weak and – extraordinary in the world of politics – have done all this without seeking fame or demanding reward. Such a figure is Wilberforce.

The Wilberforce I refer to is not the famed opponent of slavery but, rather, the fabled cat of 10 Downing Street. At least he *was* the Downing Street cat; he retired two years ago and now lives quietly in Essex. He shares his retirement home with his master, the caretaker of Number 10, Peter Taylor, Mr Taylor's family and Mr Taylor's dog, a large collie-labrador hybrid. With the diplomatic skills he learnt during his years in Whitehall, Wilberforce has had no difficulty in adjusting to this new domestic arrangement, nor in ensuring that he takes precedence over the dog for the pleasure of the morning brush-up.

However, Wilberforce, when he heard of this book, graciously consented to come up to town to show us over his old home and share with us some reminiscences of his rich political life.

Although he nurses a slight limp, the trace of an injury he received as a kitten, there is little in his forceful manner or twinkling eye to suggest that his fifteen years weigh heavily upon him. No one would describe Wilberforce as a pretty cat, but he does have the unmistakeable *gravitas* and poise of an elder statesman. When he first arrived at Downing Street as a kitten from the Hounslow RSPCA he looked, according to Mr Taylor, 'like a Staffordshire bull-terrier with a gammy leg.' Just as he has retained the traces of his vexing leg-injury, so he still bears a marked resemblance to this breed of dog.

He is very large and sturdily built. His white coat is spotted with haphazard patches of black and tabby fur, and his sizeable white head tapers to a broad, blunt nose. He is not the sort of cat one might find adorning a chocolate box. His looks are those rather of an eighteenth-century, rat-catching, tavern cat – a formidable beast.

He was named almost by default. When Peter Taylor took charge of the new and strange-looking kitten, he received a plethora of suggestions regarding its name: Had he considered Winston? 'What about Disraeli?', 'Gladstone would be rather good.' 'The cat should be called Pitt.' (not an obvious choice), 'Walpole might suit . . .'. Eventually, despairing in the face of so much helpfulness, Mr

Taylor hit upon the name Wilberforce. He happened to be passing a bust of the great man on the main staircase just as he was being pestered afresh by an over-eager member of the Disraeli lobby. 'The cat is called Wilberforce, and that's the end of it,' said Mr Taylor, stepping smartly past the dumb-struck canvasser.

Wilberforce was taken on to the Downing Street staff as a mousecatcher. During the middle years of Edward Heath's administration not the least of that Prime Minister's problems was a plague of mice infesting his home. The usual Civil Service channels had been gone through. The Department of Agriculture and Fisheries had provided some particularly unappetizing rodent-poison and a series of forms to be filled out (in triplicate) upon the demise of each mouse. The forms, however, remained untouched, as did the regulation-issue poison; the mice refused to eat it. Peter Taylor realized that direct action was called for and, to the great chagrin of the Department of Ag. and Fish., he called in Wilberforce.

Wilberforce, true to his looks, is an exemplary mouser. He is patient, watchful and tenacious. 'He always gets his mouse,' says Mr Taylor with obvious pride. One bold mouse, when cornered by Wilberforce on the first-floor landing, did attempt to escape its fate, but in vain. It leapt down the stairwell to its death and Wilberforce, untroubled, sauntered down the stairs to consume the still warm morsel at his leisure.

In the face of such a campaign of terror the Downing Street mouse community wisely decided to move. It is rumoured that they transferred themselves to the wainscots of the Home Office where the long tradition of keeping a cat, always called Peter (or sometimes, in these times of equal-opportunity recruitment, Peta), had recently come to an end.

Wilberforce, largely relieved of his mouse-catching duties, then turned his attention to charming the human population of 10 Downing Street. Initially he had been wary of people, perhaps as the result of some mistreatment he had received before his arrival at the Hounslow RSPCA, but his natural friendliness soon overcame his fears. One of his particular pleasures was taking clawed swipes at the legs of passing office girls. Most of the female staff took to keeping spare pairs of stockings in their desk drawers.

Popular with the office workers, Wilberforce was also respected by the politicians. Albert Murray, one of Harold Wilson's government advisers, was discovered sitting on the floor of his

office, surrounded by papers, while Wilberforce snored happily in his chair. When visiting dignitaries came to call at Downing Street, Wilberforce would take up a prominent position, lying across the corridor, demanding to be introduced.

Wilberforce used to have the run of the building. He would tour the offices demanding attention and food. For, after the mice moved away, Wilberforce was obliged to satisfy his prodigious appetite and exercise his formidable intelligence by coaxing titbits out of the various government departments housed at Number 10. Inter-departmental communication not being the forte of the Civil Service, Wilberforce was able to eat well and often.

At Downing Street Wilberforce was blessed not only with a fine house but also with a large and well-tended garden, a rare luxury in central London. The garden provided good hunting, a pleasant site to idle away the summer afternoons, and access into St James' Park. Although he would make occasional expeditions into the park or down the street, Wilberforce never strayed far. He had a keen sense that Number 10 was the centre of operations and that his presence there was of the utmost importance. During his years of employment he witnessed the differing regimes of four Prime Ministers.

Edward Heath, while grateful for Wilberforce's pest-control operations, always maintained a certain distance from his feline protector. Harold Wilson, on the other hand, was an intimate of Wilberforce's; they enjoyed a great deal of mutual admiration and respect. It was Harold Wilson who moved the bust of William Wilberforce from its inglorious perch on the main staircase to a dramatically-lit niche in the study antechamber.

The Wilsons, during Harold's first term at Number 10, had had a cat of their own, called Nimmo, who, however, had died by the time of their return. Nevertheless the Tory press did not lose the opportunity to invent a hurtful and wholly untrue rumour that Nimmo and the Wilsons were going to drive Wilberforce out. Such tales could scarce have been less true. Harold was devoted to Wilberforce. He would show him off to visiting world-leaders and it was he who first took Wilberforce into the Cabinet Room. James Callaghan continued cordial relations with the cat, and Mrs Thatcher, despite her affection for bulldogs, has always maintained a keen and solicitous interest in Wilberforce. It has been suggested that the tin of pilchards she was seen buying on her state trip to Russia was intended as a gift for the cat.

Wilberforce, like most cats and politicians, has a penchant for good fish, particularly cod. He was obliged to intervene personally during the troubled negotiations about the Icelandic fishing limits. As the two sides sat at Downing Street striving to bring the Cod War to an end, supplies of the precious fish were running dangerously short. Rather than face a diet of coley, Wilberforce strode into the Cabinet Room and took his place at the conference table. His calm yet insistent presence served to focus the minds of the negotiators, and an agreement was soon reached.

Although Wilberforce has always been happy to speak to the representatives of the Press he, like his Prime Ministers, has found that they sometimes overstep the mark in their demands. While he was always content to pose on the front step, he would do so only on his own terms. During the night of the 1983 General Election, Esther Rantzen, who was covering the event for the BBC from outside Number 10, asked if she could do a filler story about the cat. Peter Taylor and Wilberforce happily agreed, but were slightly put out to discover that they would have to rehearse the action first. Wilberforce went through his paces for the rehearsal but then lost patience with the escapade and, as the camera started up and Esther, beginning her spiel, opened the door of 10 Downing Street to introduce the feline star, he shot out past her and disappeared into the night.

*Woman's Own*, perhaps warned by this incident, tried to overcome the potential problem by giving Wilberforce a tranquillizer in order to slow him down for their photographer. It was not a success. Wilberforce almost fell asleep on the doorstep, and then wobbled off looking very cross.

We were happy to forego both rehearsals and tranquillizers, content instead to follow Wilberforce as he toured his old haunts, sniffing out the sites of past battles and triumphs. He seemed very happy to be back in his old house – an elder statesman drinking in the well-remembered atmosphere of political intrigue, recalling how once he chased mice down the corridors of power.

## RICHARD RUTT, BISHOP OF LEICESTER

Lucy

Richard Rutt is the knitting Bishop of Leicester, the author of *A History of Handknitting*, an expert on Korean literature, and a great lover of cats. Lucy is the bishop's cat, a solemn and svelte lilac-point Siamese, whose sleek coat and bright (if slightly squint) blue eyes belie her fourteen years.

Richard has always had cats; he was brought up amongst them. As a child he had several black cats. The first was called Blackie, the next two Bunty. Later he had Rufus, a fine ginger tom that could distinguish the sound of Richard's father's motorcar and would greet it at the door. During his years in the navy Richard had a Siamese cat called Ptolemy. Ptolemy would travel home with him on the train, wearing a collar and lead.

When Richard himself took to wearing a dog-collar and went off to Korea he continued to keep cats. He had a succession of them to keep him company in the face of the rigours of the ministry and the turmoil of the revolution. These Korean moggies were usually black-and-white but they had something of the Siamese temperament. Their names – Bernadette, Pascal, Tobi, An, Philomena – reveal Richard's eclectic interests and sympathies. Sadly most of them had very brief lives. In a country where rice is wealth and rats are a curse, the Koreans choose to rely on plentiful scatterings of rat-poison rather than on bands of cats. Many of Richard's cats died from eating poisoned rats.

The Koreans thought Richard eccentric in his regard for cats, which are considered to be crafty rascals rather than typical house pets. There is a Korean superstition that if you swallow a cat's hair you will never get to heaven. While this notion made a cat a particularly unlikely companion for a missionary, it was balanced by the Korean nickname for a European – 'cat's eyes'. Moreover, there have been a few Korean cat-lovers over the centuries. Richard has translated a beautiful poem about his kitten by Yi Kyubo (1168–1241), an early prime minister of Korea.

Happily there are very few 'rogues' for Lucy to destroy around the Bishop's Lodge, an elegant 1890s building in one of Leicester's leafier suburbs. Lucy enjoys a gentle life of oriental contemplation, occasionally interrupted by a chance encounter with the family dog, a choleric terrier who had bitten a visiting vicar moments before we arrived.

Lucy did have a brother called William but he died three years ago. The loss has prompted her towards a higher regard for humans, and she now seeks their company more than before. 'She favours

### ON OBTAINING A BLACK KITTEN

Soft and silky your plush black fur,
Big and round your deep green eyes;
Your gait is like a tiger cub's,
Your voice has terrified the rats.

  I tied a red cord round your neck
  And fed you on goldfinches.
  At first you spat and showed your claws,
  But soon you purred and waved your tail.

My house has always been a poor one,
Till now we never kept a cat;
The shameless mice ran everywhere,
Gnawing holes in all the walls.

  Nibbling away inside the clothes chests,
  Reducing everything to tatters,
  Leapt on my desk in broad daylight
  And made me upset my inkstone.

I chased them as fast as I could
To drown them in boiling water.
Of course, I never caught them:
They raced me round and round the room.

  But since you came to live with us
  The mice have had their marching orders,
  The walls are no longer in danger
  And even the larder is safe.

You have no need to seek for food
So long as you destroy those rogues.

my wife's lap,' the bishop admits. 'A woman's lap gives more room to wriggle.' Lucy's increased affection has not, however, dented her inscrutable self-possession. 'We like a lot of character in our pets,' says Richard. (He probably said the same thing to the nibbled vicar.) 'They don't have to adore us. We prefer friendship on the level.' Lucy is a very level cat.

She is fed a little every two hours, an arrangement that keeps her both happy and thin. The rest of her time is devoted to following the sun from room to room on the first floor. 'She shows an increasing disinclination to go outside,' says Richard. She will step through an open door, sniff the air and then decide against an excursion. The large garden gives her little pleasure. She suffers from the unlikely terror of being carried off by a hawk and, on her rare forays outside, will hug the garden walls rather than dash across the inviting expanse of lawn.

Lucy's other dislike is motor travel. The prospect of a journey to the bishop's cottage in Rutland brings on a bout of her 'psychological whooping cough'. Whenever she is distressed she starts to cough in an alarming manner, ceasing only when she feels her woe has been properly appreciated. Her other methods of attracting attention are more direct. When the bishop is preparing his sermons or working on diocesan business Lucy will knock the

books out of his hand or interpose herself between him and the open page.

As for the bishop's knitting, all cats assume that wool was invented for their diversion rather than for any human use – an assumption with which the bishop daringly disagrees. Despite Lucy's promptings, he has yet to turn from the creation of cardigans to the making of cat's cradles.

# Pussy

We had arranged to meet Michael Berkeley, the composer, and his cat, Pussy, at their Welsh retreat in the Powis hills. Their house is called Middle Pitts. Not the most attractive of names, perhaps, but a beautiful house in a very beautiful setting. The low, two-story stone building dates from the sixteenth century and was probably an old inn. Now the road wanders along the valley bottom, leaving Middle Pitts lost in the folds of the hills, surrounded by well-grazed fields, ancient trees and recent planting. It is a charmed spot, far removed from most people's notion of what living in the pits is like.

We knocked on the door. There was no answer and no sign of Michael. Had we got the day wrong? As we hovered on the doorstep, Pussy appeared large and ginger at the window, and beckoned to us to enter. We tried the door and went in. Pussy greeted us as old friends, sweeping us along on a tide of affection and purring. She rubbed herself about our legs, she climbed into our laps, she put us at our ease and she amused us. It was a dazzling display of natural hospitality.

Pussy is not only a brilliant hostess, she is also a beauty, a ginger tabby with eyes of the palest green – like watercress soup and cream. Her paws are white and are always moving, either gently kneading the surface she is sitting on or making expressive gestures in the air. She has an elegant white ruff, which sets off her green collar and the bell and mouse-shaped, brass name-tag which hang from it. Her tail is thick and ringed, the bands of colour becoming lighter and lighter as they approach the tip.

As we sat admiring Pussy's striking tail Michael arrived. He had just driven up from London, bringing his dog, Bear. Pussy greeted them both with her customary ease and affection. She was very pleased to see them, not least because she had been on her own for the past few days – on mouse patrol – while Michael was recording down in London.

Michael reintroduced us to Pussy who, it transpired, was a 'he', is now an 'it', but is always referred to as a 'she'. She adopted Michael and his wife, Deborah Rogers, the literary agent, arriving from over the rooftops in the garden of their Notting Hill house, and refusing to leave. She was called Pussy, partly because Michael and Deborah couldn't work out what sex she was (a position that the cat probably now finds itself in). The vet was unimpressed by their incompetence and appalled by their lack of imagination. Nevertheless he addresses his appointment cards to 'Pussy Berkeley'.

In fact, Pussy is an apt enough name for so feline a cat, and it makes a pleasant contrast to the dog called Bear. Bear, an eager-to-please young labrador, gets on well with Pussy; they play together. Bear's predecessor – a dog with the even more unlikely name of Trout – was altogether too cold a fish to enjoy romping with the cat.

As a child Michael had a succession of cats with honest, plain names – a tabby cat called Tabby, a white cat called William. Less successful was his excursion up the feline social scale; Stanford Dingley was not an easy cat. 'He got a bit above himself,' recalls Michael. 'He lacked the warmth of the London Cockney cats we'd had before then.' Michael is much happier to find himself once again with a reformed alley cat – a warm-hearted, Notting Hill-billy stray with a no-nonsense name.

Although they are both London born and bred, Michael and Pussy love the countryside. 'Like me she would rather be here all the time,' says Michael. 'In town she gets set upon by the neighbourhood males who haven't been neutered, here she is mistress of all she surveys.' While Pussy chases mice and voles, Michael likes to walk on the hills or work on the farm. He has learnt from Pussy to slow down the pace of his life in the country. She is very good company in the country. She provides a framework of routine with her regular meal-time demands. (When she is left alone at Middle Pitts the farmer comes by to feed her.) 'And in the evening she comes and sits on my lap by the fire,' says Michael.

She often chooses to leap into his lap just when he is starting work. Michael has a marvellous study at Middle Pitts, furnished with a grand piano and stunning views of the wood-clad hills and the bird-specked skies. 'There are so many birds here,' says Michael. 'There are buzzards and ravens. You can sometimes hear the ravens "honking". We also have a bird table, which brings lots of small birds but is a bit of a risk with Pussy around.' Pussy appreciates the many pleasures of Michael's study, not the least of which is Michael's lap.

Although Pussy can sometimes be rather a distraction, at the moment she is a positive inspiration. Michael is working on the music for a ballet about the Egyptian cat-goddess Bastet, to be choreographed by Lynn Seymour, designed by Andrew Logan (of Alternative Miss World infamy) and performed by the Sadler's Wells Royal Ballet. The story, like so many ballet stories, is a touching tale of fraught romance. A girl loves a boy, but discovers

that he is in love with Bastet, the cat-goddess. She asks Bastet what she should do and Bastet, with that appealing lack of false modesty common to cats and deities, transforms the girl into the very image of Bastet so that, thus disguised, she can capture her lover's heart.

Although born in West London rather than in Ancient Egypt, Pussy, like all cats, is aware that her distant ancestors were worshipped as gods on the banks of the Nile. Michael has been watching her closely, trying to capture some of her feline grace and divine aura in his ballet music. Pussy, the former stray, is more than happy to serve as a muse, especially for so noble a theme. Stanford Dingley, for all his airs, was never called upon to be the model for a divinity.

# Gizmo, Puzzle & Saijo

Ballerinas in their professional lives have more call to model themselves upon birds than upon cats. Although there are a few feline roles, the repertoire is better stocked with dying swans than jumping cats. Nevertheless Fiona Chadwick, one of the Royal Ballet's most admired principals, has always adored cats. She now has three of them.

Despite many years of distant admiration, it is only recently that she has become a cat-owner. Her mother has an irrational terror of cats, so as a child Fiona could not keep them. 'When I was about three,' she recalls, 'I brought a kitten home, and Mum had to shut herself in the lounge until it was gone.' Fiona can understand her mother's phobia. 'Some cats do look a bit scary; especially the thin ones.' Her own three cats are so plump, fluffy and affectionate that even her mother has now come to accept them. Fiona adores them.

They are pedigree Persians – Gizmo, Puzzle and Saijo. Gizmo, a three-year-old peach-coloured cream-point, is the eldest. He is a cat of extremely placid temperament and unabashed *embonpoint*. He does not believe in jumping up on to anything higher than a low sofa, a prejudice perhaps born of disinclination but now – with the steady expansion of his stately girth – confirmed by inability. Rather than overtax himself by trying to leap onto a friendly lap, he prefers to prostrate himself at the feet of his admirers, rolling over on to his back and offering his stomach to be rubbed and tickled.

Very occasionally he can be stirred to action, especially if he feels the ordered peace of his existence threatened by unwelcome change. When Fiona went on tour with the Royal Ballet, she was obliged to leave the cats with friends. Gizmo, so alarmed by his unfamiliar surroundings, shot up the chimney in an unprecedented display of energy. He did eventually come down, his light fur thick with soot, and gradually he recovered the placid equilibrium that is his natural state.

But Gizmo's reverie is tinged with sadness. Fiona acquired him along with his beloved and elegant sister. However, she was soon carried off by a mystery illness, leaving her brother grieving and alone. Fiona decided she must find him a companion. She ended up getting him two. (It should be said that Fiona had originally thought that one cat, and a mogg at that, would be quite enough altogether. She applied to Battersea and the Blue Cross but was told that there were no kittens available. Then she saw an advertisement offering two Persian kittens, Gizmo and his sister.) The next two kittens, companions for the bereft Gizmo, were irresistible bundles of fluff

in the window of a local pet-shop. 'Cats are a bit addictive,' confesses Fiona.

The arrival of two skittish kittens, Saijo and Puzzle, at first alarmed the peace-loving Gizmo but their antics soon came to amuse him, then to intrigue him and, finally, to involve him. He was rejuvenated.

Of the two young companions, Saijo is perhaps the most playful and mischievous. He is a Persian tabby and his dark hairs spread everywhere. He swings from the curtains, destroys jigsaw puzzles and rips up the bouquets that Fiona receives, strewing a litter of petals about himself.

He has the instincts of a hunter but, so far, has confined his prey to the worms from the garden. He brings them into the house, proudly laying them at the feet of his mistress. She is less than appreciative of the honour. Despite so much energy and activity, Saijo displays an engaging lack of coordination; his bold schemes sometimes overreach his imperfect agility. He often falls off the garden fence. The mischievous adventurer is also a lovable sap. His favourite position is curled upon Fiona's lap, purring loudly.

Puzzle, though very affectionate, is less inclined to sit about. She is the quickest and sharpest of the three cats, wary of strangers and well able to give as good as she gets in her games with the forceful Saijo. Puzzle, the only female, is a grey, toti-point Persian. She is very inquisitive, a trait that has not been dimmed by a near-fatal brush with the front-loading washing machine.

Fiona was just about to start the machine one morning and, having kicked the door closed, was setting the dial when she noticed Puzzle dozing amongst the dirty washing inside the tub. What cat would not assume that a warm cavern, strewn with soft materials, had been specially designed as a feline day-bed? To correct this dangerous (though understandable) misconception

Fiona gave Puzzle a once-round on the dry-spin setting before opening the door. Puzzle has not returned to the custom-made day-bed.

While Saijo loves lilies, Puzzle delights in grapes. She plays football with them, dribbling them across the floor in a frenzy of energy and concentration. Saijo's efforts to tackle her are more comical than effective.

The three cats live happily together, often sleeping in one large, multi-coloured pile of purring fur. They eat together too. Rather, Saijo and Puzzle eat first and then the gentle-natured Gizmo mops up what is left. This is perhaps a blessing to Gizmo who had become quite fat in his grief. He sought consolation in food, demolishing large platefuls of raw minced chicken in an effort to forget the loss of his dear sister. Fiona also gives each cat a bone to chew on; they are very possessive about their bones and growl like dogs if anyone threatens to take them away.

If they are all happy to improve the sheen of their coats by sucking bone marrow, they are much less keen about being brushed. Puzzle submits with silent resignation, Saijo assumes that it is a game and attacks the brush vigorously as he imagines it is trying to attack him. Gizmo hates the operation without reserve. Fiona only has to open the cupboard where the brush is kept for Gizmo to streak out of the room. Gizmo dribbles with fear at the sight of the flea-spray.

But even the uncomfortable indignities of the flea-spray are soon forgiven and forgotten, and the mood of luxuriant and playful affection reasserts itself over the trio. Although cats have apparently inspired ballets (Balanchine, I am told, used to observe his cat to gain inspiration for his choreography), it is doubtful that such feline muses were as cuddly and home-loving as Gizmo, Saijo and Puzzle.

# The Pussies

Fortune has smiled upon the Pussies. A couple of moggs transported from the sawdust of a Bermondsey pet-shop to the spacious beauties of a Scottish stately home, the Pussies have, as cats will, fallen on their feet. They are like a couple of amiable small-time London villains who, to their bemusement, have come into a country estate by a quirk of fate and are now determined to enjoy it.

Although Lady Crawford calls them the Pussies, the two cats were originally named Cat and Morris by her son's girlfriend. Cat is sleek and black, alert and aggressive, with the air of a metropolitan spiv. Morris, by contrast, belongs more to the old school, an established gang-boss to Cat's frisky hoodlum. He is built along generous lines, dressed in a well-cut black suit with distinguished white gloves and stockings. His face, broad and flattish, is brightened by unblinking green eyes which observe much but give little away; a hint of refined but submerged menace is provided by a neat black goatee that, along with his black nose, balances the white mask of his lower face. Morris endures Cat's noisome antics and petty insubordinations up to a point but, that point having been reached, he will administer a firm clout to bring the offender back into line.

Although they are not brothers, they come from the same pet-shop in Bermondsey. As kittens they presented a pathetic sight, huddled amongst the sawdust in the shop window. Poor Cat had his cage pushed up beside that of a fierce and vocal dog. He looked very unhappy. They were rescued from this grisly existence by Lady Crawford's son Alexander and his girlfriend. She bought them for him as a present. 'Poor Alex was a complete novice,' Lady Crawford recalls. 'He bought them leads and little coats and thought he would be able to take them for walks. Also they needed endless inoculations. He was always taking them to the vet. It was very expensive.'

It was also impossible to take them for walks; the pet-shop owner had been either over-optimistic or misguided in his assertion that they would enjoy being taken out on the leads. They preferred skittering around on the vast wooden floor of Alex's Bermondsey warehouse-flat. They reserved their most frenetic bouts of skating for the early hours of the morning, waking the flat with the din of their tiny claws against the sanded floorboards.

Alex's devotion to them was further tested by their habit of using his forest of potted ferns as a general litter. The delicate plants,

brought up on love, understanding and Baby Bio, were not prepared to have their diet supplemented by cat urine. They died swiftly.

But it was not this that prompted Alex to pass his disruptive pets on to his mother. The move was supposed to be merely temporary, a Scottish holiday for the cats while Alex was away filming in Afghanistan. It was not a holiday that started well. Initially they were overcome by the trauma of transportation. 'When they first arrived they were terrified of green grass and going outside.' They would sit by the kitchen window and mew to be let in. But their agoraphobia did not last. They soon developed an attachment to the gardens of Balcarres and to Lady Crawford. It is easy to see why.

Lady Crawford is an inspired gardener and she has created in the grounds of Balcarres, the ancestral seat of the Earls of Crawford since the sixteenth century, a horticultural feast. Even the most urban cat could not but be impressed by the densely planted profusion of her enclosed parterre garden, each rich bed informed by a different prevailing colour, one white, one yellow, one peach, one pink, all beautiful. And beyond the herbaceous borders are the bosky charms of the wild woodland garden, created by Lady Crawford for her grandchildren and thoughtfully planted with clumps of greatly appreciated and much revelled-in catnip.

The cats may love the garden but they also love the gardener; they even enjoy gardening. Lady Crawford has only to set out with her trug for them to appear at her heels. They spring on to her shoulders when she is weeding and climb along the beams of the fruit cage if she is picking raspberries.

'They seem to have taken a great liking to me,' Lady Crawford says in a tone tinged with amazement. 'So I like them. And now when Alex (safely returned from Afghanistan) comes here, does he show any feeling for them? Not at all.' But the Pussies don't seem to mind. The Balcarres acres hold many more opportunities for them than the expanses of Alex's studio.

Lady Crawford's daughter, Iona, is sure that her mother is 'trying to turn the cats into vegetarians', feeding them the leftovers from the castle table – 'salad, potatoes, everything.' Nevertheless the Pussies are never short of meat as they not only get tinned cat-foot but also have a large estate to hunt. Their London street wisdom has been happily transferred to the rural setting. They have already taken a brace of pheasants this season.

Although Lady Crawford professes to be surprised to find herself with cats, it transpires that she did buy the long-lived and much-loved family cat that preceded the Pussies. She paid £1 for a ginger kitten at a constituency bazaar when her husband was an MP. This cat, called Puss, was a great success, loved by the children and living for twenty-two years.

He even survived several days lost in Coventry, a fate that might have carried off many humans. He had rashly climbed out of the

fractionally open car-window when the family, heading south from Scotland to London, had stopped off to visit the cathedral. On their return to the car-park there was no sign of Puss and apparently very little hope of ever finding him again. He was, however, reunited with them several days later after they had given details of him to the local RSPCA. Puss had seemed less distressed by the ordeal than the family were.

Between Puss' death and the arrival of Alex's cats Lady Crawford was happy to live without pets. 'My friends are always saying, "What, you have no dogs in the country?" They think I am a very strange specimen.' But how could she turn away the cats of a son heading towards a war zone; how could she resist the attentions of animals who took such frank delight in her delightful garden? As she says, 'It always turns out happily. Once I have cats I do really like them.'

# Tabitha

'Tabitha does love people but I am afraid she is rather inclined to gush,' warned Honora Miles as she introduced me to her very self-assured, thick-haired tortoiseshell-tabby cat. Tabitha was obviously on her best behaviour, or else she was less than bowled over by my arrival. She was welcoming without overstatement and attentive without ever going so far as to gush. With a consideration rare in cats, for the requirements of photography Tabitha strolled out of the front door and stood in the garden, striking various fetching poses in the morning sunlight.

Tabitha, known as Tablets, lives with Honora at Aughnagaddy in Donegal. It is a house of great charm and mild eccentricity, a low and ancient rectory built around an internal court- (or rather, farm-) yard. It has, like so many Irish houses, endured an exhausting history. The earliest parts of the building date from the sixteenth century. By the beginning of the 1800s the house had blossomed into an impressive three-storey edifice, but this large and rather unsophisticated pile was not considered to be of a style worthy of an Irish rector's dignity. So in the 1820s an elegant, if square, Georgian house was built beside the old house, which was stripped of its third storey and filled up with difficult relations. The Georgian box did not last out the century. It was burnt down and the old house was reclaimed. Alterations were made; a stone staircase was installed and the site of the burnt rectory was turned into a tennis court.

Honora shares the house with her sister Araminta. Araminta and her husband live downstairs among the oriental artefacts and exotic hunting trophies which the sisters' father, an army surgeon, brought back from his sojourn in the East. Honora and Tabitha live above in a fairy-tale world of antique dolls. There are dolls everywhere, sitting on nursery chairs, perched on tables, lolling on couches, some with solemn porcelain brows and tiny cupid's-bow mouths, others with long, soft eyelashes and cheery smiles.

One room contains an impressive urban settlement of three splendid doll's houses, ranging in style from Irish Georgian to 1920s suburban. Each house is alive with drama and wit – and cats. In one richly-decorated drawing-room, a many-petticoated Spanish lady gossips with an Indian princess while a large and fluffy white cat sprawls in front of the glowing fire and looks indolently at a nervous mouse across the carpet. On the roof a black alley-cat yowls at the moon.

Tabitha herself has a very impressive yowl. Honora describes it as

'a jungly voice' and thinks she must have learnt it from a neighbouring peacock, or perhaps from the shades of the jungly animals whose heads adorn the walls downstairs. Although thoroughly domestic and indeed refined, Tabitha would certainly not disgrace a jungle. She has the stocky frame and thick, ringed tail of a wild cat. Her dense and multi-coloured coat has lost little of its sheen over a long life, and her face is remarkable not only for its contented aspect but also for its distinguished white chin and arresting malachite eyes.

Tabitha arrived at Aughnagaddy over twenty years ago. She was a child of the Troubles, born in the Bogside area of Derry in 1968 as the 'first bangs' of dissension shattered the evening's peace. Tabitha's heavily-pregnant mother, alarmed by the noise, climbed into a house through an open window and gave birth under the kitchen table. Two of this litter of kittens came across the border to Aughnagaddy, Tabitha and her late brother Tom, a big black

tom-cat (although, of course, then he was a little Tom Kitten).

Honora needed cats. 'The mice had been getting out of hand,' she says with a trace of regret. 'They wouldn't even look up when you came into the room. But although the cats came as mousers they were soon running the whole place.'

It was Tabitha who was the most demanding and the strongest-willed. She would, however, let Tom wash and groom her as a mark of favour. Honora reckons that 'Tablets doesn't know she is a cat, she has lived with people for so long.' While it seems unlikely that a cat would ever be deluded enough to suppose itself to be a creature as base as a mere person, Tabitha does display an attractive directness in her dealings with humans: there is not a hint of condescension in her manner.

She is less generous to fellow cats. Tom, of course, was loved as a brother but other felines are regarded as rivals and ruffians. The countryside around the rectory supports several half-wild strays who sometimes appear in the garden on food-raids. Tabitha does not welcome them. And when a friend's grey cat came to stay for a few days, Tabitha sat crossly inside a paper bag for the duration of the visit.

Guest dogs are, surprisingly, less disturbing; Tabitha has tamed many dogs to her will, standing her ground and staring them down with an imperious gleam in her bright green eyes. Part of her confidence comes from having been brought up with a dog. When Coco; Honora's King Charles spaniel died in 1982, Tabitha fell into a depression and went off her food. They had been very close, grooming each other, sharing a favoured chair and playing tag together.

While Tabitha does not play with the farmyard birds and animals, neither does she chase them. The ducks and chickens in the yard happily ignore her and the two horses seem positively friendly. 'They're lap horses really,' explains Honora. 'They've never been properly broken for riding.'

And, of course, there are the dolls. Tabitha ignores most of the antique dolls propped upon their chairs and sofas about the house but she is intrigued by the beautiful doll's houses. She used to 'haunt' the elegant drawing-room of the fine late-Georgian doll's house, squeezing through the french windows and curling up in front of the fire. Each morning Honora would find the room empty but all the dolls and their furniture overturned and pushed against the wall. She feared that the house, made in Dublin at the beginning of the nineteenth century, might have come complete with a poltergeist, but such thoughts were stilled when, one morning, she discovered Tabitha crammed into the drawing-room, her face filling the french window.

Tabitha, as a hunter herself, has an admiration for the various eastern game-trophies on the walls of the ground floor. There is a

striking photograph of her perched on the gigantic bison's head that greets you with unwavering eye as you walk through the front door. Honora showed the picture to the local butcher who was much impressed. 'Where did you get that bull?' he asked in awe. He has given Tabitha free meat ever since.

Tabitha still enjoys catching some extra free meat on her own account. She has never forgotten that she was taken on as a mouser. She has extended her range to include rabbits, 'the occasional drop-in robin' and any feckless bats. For her, as for most of Ireland, hunting is a serious business, not to be treated with undue levity. Therefore you can imagine Tabitha's disdain for a kind but ill-considered gift recently received. A well-intentioned guest presented her with a garishly-coloured pink toy-mouse, complete with bell. 'I'm afraid she won't touch it,' Honora says approvingly. 'A pink mouse with a bell – what extraordinary bad taste.'

# Snowy & Patch

Punctuality is not always a characteristic of railway companies, but it is a virtue found even less often in railway company cats. We had made an appointment for 11.00 am to meet Snowy, the station cat at Bristol Temple Meads. Eleven o'clock passed with no sign of the cat. There was not even an announcement over the public-address system to apologise for the delay and to suggest when the cat might be due in. The platform staff, though courteous and understanding, could offer little concrete information. Snowy would arrive, but they couldn't say when. There was nothing for it but to wait. Our vigil was not an easy one: the consoling splendour of Brunel's edifice was offset by the chill of the platform, the doubt as to whether Snowy would ever arrive ('He sometimes goes off for days at a time.') and the fear of being mistaken for train-spotters.

The station at Bristol Temple Meads has a long association with cats. Before Snowy there was a famous cat, known variously as Tops (after the acronym for a newly installed train monitoring system) and Whisky (he was black and white). Tops was born at a nearby shunting yard which was closed down soon afterwards. The young cat was taken home by one of the redundant railwaymen to a suburb on the fringes of Bristol. Railways, however, were in Tops' blood. He ran away from home and reappeared at Temple Meads several weeks later. He lived on until the age of fourteen, amusing the passengers, charming the staff and making regular appearances on local television. He had obviously been more attuned to the needs of the media than the still invisible Snowy.

As we shivered on the platform a kindly porter told us that Snowy was not the only cat at Temple Meads. There was another one, called Patch, down in the Red Star Parcels office. The words 'parcels office' conjured up a vision of cardboard-lined warmth and cosiness; the word 'cat' seemed happily apt as well. We hurried off.

Patch, the Red Star cat, was not in his office when we arrived. He was playing amongst the wire-caged parcel trolleys. Patch, as his name might suggest, is covered in patches. Depending upon your perspective he is a white cat with black patches – or vice versa. He was found shivering on the parcel-office steps one morning over a year ago. He had an injured leg. Now he is firmly ensconced, admired and petted by all. He spends most of his day dozing in the warmth of the 'inner sanctum', the main administration office, but at night he hunts for mice in the vaults under the station platforms. He seldom ventures far on his hunting trips and only very rarely spends a night away. He has access to the 'inner sanctum' at all

times via an impromptu cat-flap made from a sliding
ticket-window.

Patch is a good friend of Snowy's. They often breakfast together
in the parcels office and then fritter away an hour playing tag
amongst the wire trolleys. Patch has recovered from his leg injury
and, although he sometimes shows a slight awkwardness in sitting
down, is a very frolicsome cat, full of japes and jests.

We were admiring Patch's sprightly antics when, sensing no doubt that the moment was both dramatic and propitious, Snowy made his belated appearance. He was worth the wait. Snowy is black, very black and very beautiful. He is small and lithe, with a handsome head and lustrous green eyes. Despite a fabled appetite he shows no trace of fat – or worms. His coat shines with good health and ripples over his well-muscled frame.

Snowy is on the BR pay bill and has regular meals at the staff canteen. He has also become adept at playing the intricate British Rail bureaucracy to his advantage. Safe in the knowledge that one administrative department has no idea what another is doing, he wanders about the station offices claiming regular meals from each of them, and assuring them all of his especial love, loyalty and dependence. He even calls by for a bacon sandwich from the taxi-drivers' café in the station forecourt. He does, however, earn his wages (and further supplement his diet) by catching numerous mice and occasional pigeons in and about the station. He has something of a wild streak and sometimes disappears on safari for long periods of time.

During the day, when not visiting his benefactors or playing with Patch, Snowy patrols his fief, observing the smooth running of the great station from a variety of vantage points. Often he is to be found sitting on the long counter in the ticket hall, watching, through slitted eyes, the people buying their tickets. On chill days he prefers to sprawl across two comfortable seats in the new, and warm, Travel Centre.

Although Snowy likes being around people, he is wary of being picked up. He is affectionate and courteous but always aware of his dignified position as a BR employee. 'I've seen some people smooth him,' says one of the porters, 'but I've seen him go for people too.'

Snowy, like his predecessor Tops, was born in a shunting yard. He came as a young kitten from Avonmouth, arriving at Temple Meads by train. He has not lost his appreciation of railway travel. Not infrequently he disappears up to Manchester or Birmingham on the train, or makes local excursions on the branch lines. He has a particular fondness for the Glasgow sleeper. This train stands in the station for over an hour with most of its doors open, allowing for easy and unhurried access, and it has the added virtue of a well-stocked buffet car. Fortunately for Snowy's many Bristol friends (from Patch down to the station master) and, of course, for himself, he always remembers to buy a return ticket.

# Estella, Flake, Serafina,

David Vicary, architect, interior- and garden-designer, arbiter of taste and man of discernment, lives in a crumbling parsonage set in a tangled garden, deep in the wilds of Wiltshire. His numerous cats perhaps take their cue more from this untended setting than from the refined creations of their master's professional work. But, just as one can still glimpse the once choice and ordered planting of the now riotously overgrown gardens and admire the still fine outlines of the Georgian stone house (built by Wood the Elder, one of the creators of Bath), so one can see still the varieties of feline grace in David Vicary's delightful assortment of frisky, tumbled-up cats.

David has six cats at the moment; three whites, one tabby and two blacks. He has always had several white cats since he received his first white kitten from Corsham in 1969. The kitten, named Flake White, was the first of a succession of 'odd-eyed, short-haired, white common cats'. At one moment David had seven of them. 'I can't bear to get rid of them,' he explains. 'They breed on the radiator in my bedroom.' Sadly feline leukaemia has carried off many, but there are always new kittens jostling for position on the radiator.

The current collection of cats comprises the beautiful Estella and her numerous offspring. Estella, known also in more formal circles as Mrs Tootington Smiley, and among her bohemian friends as Toot, is an odd-eyed, pure white, ten-year-old beauty. She has a very pretty head, with a shelving, leonine profile. David suspects that Estella's eighteenth-century ancestors provided the model for the heraldic lion's head used for hallmarks. Estella's regal, or reginal, bearing certainly does nothing to dispel the notion.

Toot is used to being admired; she was photographed by Snowdon for *Vogue* when he was doing a feature on the house. She is also used to being obeyed. If the other cats step out of line, she administers a terse rebuke backed up with a deft clout.

Despite the natural poise she now displays, Estella had a troubled start in life. Like her Dickensian namesake, she was found in a ditch. Estella's mother was called Flake, after the founder of the line. There have been four Flakes over the years; this particular one, perhaps disturbed by her pregnant state, ran off to live wild. David spent several anxious days calling for her in the fields, and was on the point of despairing when the sounds of insistent mewing drew him to a damp but sheltered ditch where he found three white kittens, abandoned and afraid. He gathered them up and brought them home. Estella was the prettiest, her sister, Rosa Blanchfleur,

# Balthassare Carlos, Objet & Phantom

was 'a big bag of nerves', while her brother, the third Flake, 'was very trusting and friendly, as toms are.'

Only Estella remains of this foundling trio but she is now surrounded by her variegated progeny. She has two white-haired children – the fourth Flake and the even-eyed Serafina. Flake is a gentle four-year-old tom, who has recently been driven off his territory by Phantom, the young tabby. David does not believe in doctoring his cats and, although for the most part they all get on happily, there is often trouble between the males after two or three years. Flake now lives wild (or comfortably with charitable neighbours – David is unsure) and rarely returns to the Parsonage. Serafina, on the other hand, seldom leaves it. She is a twin to the sleek black Balthassare Carlos and they make a fine sight walking together with their tails crossed. She adores her mother and is happy to live in her shadow.

The two black cats are so skittish that they seldom sit still long enough to cast a shadow. Balthassare Carlos is marginally less febrile than the young Objet who is forever on the hop. 'He is very hoppity-skippity,' complains David. 'So difficult to work with.' Their colouring comes from the nearby black farm-cats, as does their nature, which is alert, predatory and mischievous. 'They have a very acute sense of smell. You can't hide anything from them. They once stole some steak from the boot of the car of some friends who were visiting.'

Phantom, the two-year-old tabby, is the dominant male of the moment. 'He's a very charming chap, very matey,' sais David. 'We talk a great deal. And when he returns from an expedition he sings to me. He is very flat. He is a wonderful cat, but all he can think about is food.' When we arrived to visit, Phantom was the only cat not to come and greet us. He was engrossed, feasting noisily on a freshly-slaughtered rabbit under the holly tree.

The tangled jungle of the garden provides a wealth of prey for the cats. 'They hunt squirrels, rabbits and long-tailed tits, alas.' David tries to discourage them from eating birds, but it is difficult. 'One ageing bullfinch flew straight into Flake's mouth while he was yawning!' Although David and the cats are content to ignore the roe deer that occasionally appear at the door, they are less keen on the local foxes. Recently they lost a young black kitten, Busby Berkeley, to a marauding vixen.

David now takes care to keep the kittens inside. For the most part, however, his cats are allowed to roam free. Although the

garden is surrounded by fields, the cats seldom venture beyond the limits of their own private, tangled woodland. Like dogs they come when David calls them, and they even accompany him for a while if he is walking into town. But beyond these instances of dog-like devotion, they are a very feline collection – wilful, individualistic and independent.

Much of their strength of character doubtless arises from their distinctive names. David spends up to six months observing a new kitten before deciding upon a name for it. The white cats all have names suggestive of whiteness, brightness and light; apart from the current crop, past favourites include Bonifazio (after a white-washed village in Corsica) and Blanche. Cats of other shades and colourings are named according to their natures. The cats, of course, appreciate and delight in the fact that, while the gardening is left untended, the vital business of their christening is given such just and careful consideration. It is, they think, as it should be.

# Posy & Christabel

Lady Abdy lives surrounded by Sèvres porcelain and Persian cats. It is a daring combination, but one that shows a keen regard for elegance and beauty above the mundane considerations of mere caution. Accidents, in fact, are happily rare; Sèvres is made from a heavier paste than most porcelain and Posy and Christabel, the blue-cream Persians that share Jane Abdy's Belgravia home, are made of softer stuff than most cats.

They are two gorgeous bundles of luxuriant grey-bright fur, prone to merriment, minor mischief and much lolling about on blue-upholstered furniture. (Cats are, apparently, very fond of the colour blue.) Posy is named after Posy Tennant, a nineteenth-century beauty and one of the Souls, a group of aristocratic intellectuals about which Lady Abdy has written an acclaimed book. Christabel takes her name from Christabel Abercromby, a friend and author of *The Dictionary of Cat Lovers*.

With such illustrious namesakes it is little wonder that the two cats wear such an air of distinction, one heightened by their knowledge that they are the only cats in the street. 'They love London life,' says Jane. 'They prefer it to the country. Here they

have a cosy house and a pleasant garden.' Indeed they have the freedom of all the back gardens. Although they sometimes climb the cherry trees to catch birds they expend most of their energy chasing each other, playing ping pong and wrestling with a catnip mouse. 'They don't have very advanced tastes in recreation,' Jane admits. Posy loves knocking milk-cartons off the kitchen table.

They are both devoted to Jane, just as she is to them. 'I have a great bond with Posy and Christabel,' she says. 'We get on terribly well. They're very optimistic and cheerful. I like their playfulness and their contentment in doing nothing.' In a house rich with beautiful things Posy and Christabel are amongst the most beautiful. They put a good deal of time and effort into looking ornamental, grooming themselves carefully, choosing suitable backdrops for their colouring and striking languorous attitudes with their limbs. For this they expect admiration and praise.

Posy, who wears a rather worried look on her flat face, is perhaps the most demanding. 'She is totally sweet,' says Jane. 'She hates to be left alone and follows me everywhere.' She even sits on the edge of the bath when Lady Abdy is bathing, though she is careful not to get wet. Christabel on the other hand has a singular passion for recently-emptied bath tubs. She lies in the steep-sided trough of the still-warm bath, purring happily.

Posy, 'when very merry', jumps on to Jane's shoulders while she is writing or talking on the telephone. 'She will sit on your book if it is very important,' says Jane. 'She also likes sitting on the *Financial Times*.' Apparently she is not attracted to its editorial content or its fetching colour, but to the extreme softness of the paper.

The cats hate it when Jane goes away for any length of time. As soon as they see a suitcase being packed they are plunged in gloom. They take up positions on the stairs and sit staring at Jane with great, sad eyes. She can scarcely bear to leave. Yet, despite their love for Jane, the cats are not very social. Whenever Jane gives a party they take refuge in two rustic baskets downstairs on the kitchen table. Or, if one of the guests has arrived in a fur coat, they might, if it is a very choice pelt, bed down on that.

Their taste for luxury extends to food. 'Persian cats have such sweet natures,' Jane explains 'because they have been spoilt for over three thousand years.' As an historian, she is alive to the continuity of tradition and has not stinted to confirm the expectations of Christabel and Posy. They have fresh fish for breakfast (small wonder that they come to wake her up each morning) and roast chicken for supper. The cats, like Jane, do not eat red meat.

Life in Belgravia surrounded by French art and Italian furniture has given Posy and Christabel recherché tastes. 'Posy loves avocado pears,' says Jane. 'And both of them are very fond of pasta and of cheese, especially mozzarella.' As Lady Abdy puts it, 'They're real five-star luxury-loving cats.'

# Sulaka, Pushpa & Magnificat

Westminster Abbey can boast many famous treasures and splendid pleasures but, while all tourists flock happily past Poets' Corner and through King Henry's Chapel, only the discerning few pause to admire the three beautiful white cats that flit amongst the greenery of the Abbey cloisters or frolic in the sheltered expanse of the Abbey garden like angels flitting over the fields of Elysium (well, a bit like that).

The three cats belong to Canon Charles and his family. Canon Charles is a reluctant cat-lover and it is his wife and children who look after the three cats, Sulaka, Pushpa and Magnificat – or Niffi for short. Among all London's cats, few can have such handsome surroundings and such ample space as these three. Their especial domain is the old Abbey Garden, a large, walled garden hidden away behind the abbey, fringed with rich borders and dominated by massive plane trees.

All three cats love flowers; lilies in particular they adore. Inside the house they gently ravage arrangements of cut flowers, knocking petals to the floor and smudging their noses with pollen. Outside, the ornamental cherry trees provide welcome perches throughout the year, but in the spring the cats are highly and happily conscious of how fine they look stretched out upon a blossom-heavy bough, their white fur bright amongst the pink-tinged flowers. The appeal of the trees, however, is not merely aesthetic. Niffi and Pushpa, who are brother and sister, use the branches as cover when, working in concert, they attempt to catch pigeons. They are only too successful. They make a point of giving special pigeon-hunting displays for the education and edification of the current litter of kittens. (Both Pushpa and Sulaka are prodigiously fertile.)

The Abbey Garden not only has to be patrolled for pigeons but also defended against canine incursions. Officially dogs are not allowed but the rule, to the cats' chagrin, is laxly enforced and so, as concerned members of the close, they sometimes find themselves obliged to take the law into their own paws. Visiting dogs are confronted fearlessly. The last Dean had what Mrs Charles describes as 'a square, soft dog'. It was seen off by the cats on the few occasions it ventured onto their turf.

People on the other hand are treated with great courtesy and attention. They are allowed – nay, encouraged – to admire and stroke the guardians of the grove. When parties of choirboys come to sketch in the garden during the summer, the cats pose for them with gracious tolerance. When a television film about Winston Churchill was being made in the Abbey Garden, Sulaka, who at nine is the oldest of the three cats, insisted on appearing in the scene to the horror of the continuity girl. The director despaired of deflecting Sulaka's thespian energies and was forced to perpetrate the unlikely fiction that Churchill, during his war-time administration, was followed around by a pet white cat.

Privileged though their cloistered life is, the three white cats are not ignorant of the outside world. At the bottom of the garden there is a hole in the wall where a succession of tattered but virile stray tom cats have made their home. They have made their sport in the garden, fathering a line of vigorous though motley litters upon Sulaka and Pushpa. Amongst the chaste confines of the Abbey buildings it is delightful to find such fecundity. When we visited the Charleses, Pushpa was nursing three young kittens and Sulaka was heavily pregnant. When they both have litters at the same time they willingly help to look after each other's kittens.

Niffi too is fond of children. He is a splendid uncle, looking

magnificent in his long-haired coat and extravagant side-whiskers. He plays along with his kittenish nieces and nephews and is thoroughly abashed when he forgets his own strength and cuffs a kitten too hard. Dignity, however, must be maintained. Niffi refuses (rather like Yul Brynner in *The King and I*) to allow the kittens to get onto a higher level than himself. If they are scrambling up the kitchen-steps he will gently swipe them down as they try to pass the height of his head.

Sulaka, it is agreed, has the prettiest kittens. She is also the best mother. She is very calm and understanding, both towards her offspring and the people around her. When Ashok, the youngest son of the family, was very small Sulaka tolerated his clumsy attentions, deftly directing him with her paw. He benefited from growing up amongst her kittens, absorbing some of the feline sense of grace and balance. He was able to walk at eight months. Pushpa, agile and quick, is more nervous of maternity. When her kittens are due she sneaks off to have them in the privacy of Tagore's room. All three cats adore Tagore, the eldest son. He feeds them, talks to them and whistles for them. They, in turn, watch over him.

Each litter always produces at least one white kitten. The other babes come in a variety of fetching patchworks. All of them find happy homes, even the few white kittens that are born deaf. It is uncertain why white cats are more susceptible to deafness than others but the gravity of the disability is lessened by the acuteness of the animals' sense of smell and their sensitivity to vibrations. Indeed it often takes Mrs Charles some time to discover which kittens are deaf, so easily do they keep up with their siblings.

When Philip Larkin's memorial service was held in the Abbey, a visiting jazz musician who had come to play at the occasion was captivated by a little ginger kitten of Pushpa's. He took it home and has named it Larkin. Most of Sulaka's and Pushpa's kittens get named Abbey or Minster by their new owners.

All of these cloister-bred cats cannot but be imbued with some of the peace and harmony of their birthplace and some of the grace, beauty and domesticity of their mothers (and uncle). White cats are famous home-lovers but few can have had such a home to love as Sulaka, Pushpa and Niffi, the white cats of Westminster Abbey.

# Jumbo & Nutkin

John Brookes, the noted landscape-designer and author, lives in an elegantly converted flint-and-brick stable block, surrounded by the profuse planting of Denmans Garden, which he runs. It is a pleasant three-and-a-half-acre site set at the foot of the South Downs, sheltered yet open, densely planted yet delightfully unregimented. John Brookes is assisted in his work not only by several dedicated gardeners but also by two enthusiastic cats – Jumbo and Nutkin.

Jumbo and Nutkin are sisters, Jumbo is black and plump, her sister tortoiseshell and solid. The twin stars of Jumbo's character are friendliness and laziness; a warm lap is her delight. We discovered her stretched out happily on top of the water-heater, a study of contentment in black fur and white enamel. 'She has a great big stomach which she likes to have tickled,' explained John. Jumbo obligingly rolled onto her back to display the said stomach and offer us the opportunity of tickling it.

Nutkin is more reserved. She is richly turned out in a dense tortoise-shell coat, made, like her sister's, from long, thick hair, suggesting a sub-Persian origin. She has neat white paws and a white front, offset by an inky black nose and a piratical black eye-patch.

John took up with the cats when he first came to Denmans some eight years ago. They arrived as kittens from Kew and so were accustomed to living in the shade of fine plants. At first they were obliged to live in a caravan, while the stable block was being converted for habitation. But with the gardens to play in they did not complain.

The cats have maintained their interest in the gardens and during the summer they escort John on his rounds of inspection and assist him in his work. On their own, however, they do not wander far. They make brief excursions to the catnip patch for an intoxicating roll, but otherwise prefer to loiter on the warm and sheltered patio outside John's kitchen windows. This paved and planted corner catches and holds the sun, and the three large bronze geese which decorate it heat up over a sunny day, providing perfect perches for comfort-loving cats. Hidden away on the patio the cats can enjoy some privacy and calm. 'From the end of March to October the garden is open to the public and there is too much going on out there,' explains John, gesturing towards the main body of the garden. 'What with all the visitors and gardeners, the cats won't venture forth until the evening when it's dead quiet.'

Although the cats do like to go on an evening prowl, they are not

great hunters. 'A local Jack Russell used to hunt for rabbits in the garden, and it rather put them off.' What they do enjoy is climbing up the trees. Jumbo perhaps overreached herself at this sport. She once disappeared for several days and was found, cowering upstairs in the house, lame in her back legs. After a week of treatment with the vet she did regain the use of her limbs. John suspects that she fell awkwardly from a height, incurring a partial and temporary paralysis. Happily she still enjoys a climb, although she is less agile and adventurous than she was.

The cats' wariness of the crowds of visitors and troops of gardeners is not the result of misanthropy; both Nutkin and Jumbo are very fond of people. They particularly enjoy the company and attention of the students who come to attend the landscape-design summer schools run by John. 'Jumbo and Nutkin love the students, who, of course, spoil them rotten,' says John.

Although the cats take obvious pleasure in the garden at Denmans, they are not great respecters of the business of garden design. John's drawingboard they regard as a thoughtfully-provided sunbed, smooth and warm beneath the glare of the anglepoise lamp. John, with the patience of a true gardener, remains unfazed by the presence of a cat in the middle of his latest design, by the wet paw prints over his planting notes, by the litter of cat hair amongst his pens. 'These are the hazards of the cat,' as he puts it.

However, these feline hazards are balanced by the feline virtues. 'I've always liked cats. All that demonstrativeness of dogs is rather tiresome; they never give up. But cats are quietly affectionate, which I like – and they look after themselves. They don't have to be taken for walks every ten minutes. Frankly I don't have the time for all that.' Moreover, the two cats are able to keep each other company, a particular virtue, as John travels a great deal, giving lectures, holding seminars and designing gardens in distant lands.

Jumbo and Nutkin get on well together, although Nutkin defers to her fat sister. Jumbo always eats first, and if she wants the prime position on John's lap, Nutkin will make room. Often, however, they will sit harmoniously on either arm of John's armchair. At least once a day they have 'a good rough and tumble', scrabbling noisily around on the smooth, flagged floor of John's studio. But such romps are entirely without malice. As John remarks, 'They are really quite fond of each other but, like most brothers or sisters, they don't always let on.'

# Pushkin

There have always been enclaves of Russian expatriates scattered through the Royal Borough of Kensington, so it comes as no surprise to discover a cat called Pushkin living in a large stucco-fronted house in one of the borough's broader and more gracious streets. Nevertheless, neither Pushkin nor his mistress, the painter Romana McEwen, are even remotely Russian. Pushkin, despite his name, is Scottish and Romana, despite hers, is English.

Pushkin received his name because he is a black and white cat. Not only does the name approximate to the diminutive term of affection, Pusskin, but it also makes an oblique and ingenious reference to the little-known fact that Pushkin, the Russian poet, had some black blood in his veins. Pushkin, the cat, seems largely unmoved by considerations of literary biography. His facial markings – black ears, mask and nose, above a white face – give him a slight resemblance to Batman.

His origins are, however, less obscure than those of the Caped Crusader. He came from a shepherd living near the McEwans' house in Ayrshire. He was recommended by the shepherd as being a 'kitten of great character', and the McEwens felt very pleased to have received so special a beast. Some days later, however, Mrs McWhirter, who had come in from the village to do some sewing, greeted the young kitten fondly as 'Frederick'. It transpired that Frederick (or Pushkin) had been born in the village and given to the shepherd, who wanted a young kitten to keep his old cat company. Upon Frederick/Pushkin's arrival the shepherd's cat had promptly and unexpectedly produced a litter of kittens and the shepherd, thinking that mother and child would make a happier pair, had off-loaded the second-hand Frederick on to the McEwans. Nevertheless, even the discovery of this minor deceit could not dim the affection already flourishing between Romana and the cat.

'I think the children thought that I was a raving neurotic,' she says, 'and that Pushkin would produce a level of stability.' The infant Pushkin, however, had other ideas. One of his first actions *chez* McEwen was to bring the family's massive, tinsel-clad Christmas tree crashing to the ground. 'It sounded like an atom bomb going off – a strange whooshing noise and then a great crash.' The incident itself was not calculated to have a calming influence on either Romana or the cat, but the shock of the crash did produce in Pushkin a dislike of loud noises. To this day he preserves an aversion to loud music, horror films on television and family rows.

Romana is now full of praise for Pushkin's 'stabilizing' qualities.

She finds him endlessly amusing; the dead-pan humour with which he seats himself on the laps of professed cat-haters, or his boundless pleasure in playing games. There are baskets of corks all over the house, ready for his amusement. 'I like the dissembling of cats,' says Romana. 'They start whistling or washing in the middle of stalking a cork. They let you know that they realize that the game is merely a pretence. They even manage to suggest that the whole game is entirely for your benefit. They are only playing it to amuse you.'

Pushkin, while never abandoning his feline egocentricity, is very considerate of his mistress. If she has been out for the evening, he waits for her by the door. He does, however, become exceedingly vexed when Romana goes abroad. On her return from a long trip Pushkin refuses to greet her or talk about her travels. He cuts her in her own hallway. But later in the warmth of her bedroom, with great condescension he allows himself to melt. On most evenings he likes to see her safely to her bed before he goes out for a midnight prowl. 'He loves it when I have flu and he knows I will be in bed the whole time. Cats like to protect you and then desert you.'

'Pushkin was very understanding when Rory, my husband, died. He went and sat between the pillows on our bed,' she remembers fondly, before adding. 'It was probably warmer there.'

Having settled Romana in her bed for the night, Pushkin likes to take a a turn around the neighbourhood. Although he sometimes goes out the front, the street is thick with brutal dogs. 'It's a very doggy street,' laments Romana. One neighbour has two large, unspecified horrors, which he walks in the street. 'He says they're frightfully soppy but they're probably trained as killers: one gulp and – poor Pushkin.' Pushkin wisely prefers the back garden. 'It's like a private jungle out there.'

There are some other cats in the jungle, and after Romana received a midnight visit from a strange black cat, which gave her a great shock by jumping on to her bed and reduced Pushkin to a quivering wreck under the dressing-table, she installed a remote-controlled, electronic cat-flap for Pushkin's sole use. Sadly something has gone wrong with the mechanism and, after Romana discovered Pushkin pathetically bashing his nose against the stubbornly closed flap, she has had to dismantle it. The local cat population, however, has been warned off and Romana and Pushkin can now rest easy in their beds.

Pushkin certainly requires free access in and out of the house. He

complains loudly if he gets wet or finds himself on the wrong side of a door. 'Cats do complain,' says Romana, 'but they never grovel. They are much subtler than dogs; there is none of that tail-wagging and panting.'

One subject about which Pushkin makes frequent complaints and demands is food. Rory McEwen used to say, 'The trouble with that cat is he is only interested in food.' Although Pushkin might protest that he also enjoys companionship, liberal affection, playing with corks and distressing asthmatics, he would not deny that food is a subject very close to his heart.

He is fed on the best fish and liver. He is a great fan of Sainsbury's coley portions and he is known by name in Kerniks, the butcher just round the corner.

Important though good food is, Pushkin also relishes attention. He takes great pleasure in knocking things off tables and bookshelves; he knows he will get a good reaction for a very modest outlay of effort. In the McEwens' house in Ayrshire one of Pushkin's favourite japes was knocking books off a shelf in one of the bedrooms onto the sleeping people below. He never failed to gain their attention.

When Romana is working furiously in the face of some fast-approaching deadline, Pushkin, enjoying the atmosphere of mounting pressure, delights in distracting her. First he will knock over the ink bottle, then butt his head against Romana's paintbrush before, finally, sitting down in the middle of her picture.

The middle of the picture is undoubtedly where Pushkin sees himself. Certainly he is the centre of the McEwen household; he even receives personal letters. Romana refuses to consider selling the house, large as it is, because it would be too distressing for Pushkin. Her accountant despairs, but then he is not a cat-lover and cannot be expected to understand such matters. As Romana's son Adam says, 'This house is run around that cat.'

# Farm Cats

Ernie Morrow and his brother Stewart farm in the glen where they were born and bred. Set amongst the green, green hills of Glenarm their farm looks out across the land of County Antrim. The two brothers' farmhouse is a collection of low white-washed stone buildings; their home on one side and their barns on the other mark out the limits of a farmyard open to the view (and the weather) at each end.

The farmyard – and the Morrows – are both full of life and colour. As Ernie regaled us with tales of getting into fearful scrapes, of being chased by a thunderbolt and of making a rare excursion over to England to see Danny La Rue, the yard danced with the bluster of indignant cockerels, flustered ducks, and the sly presence of a limping sheep-dog who was keeping his paw in by rounding up the birds.

In the lush green, Irish grass at one end of the yard a mother cat was playing with her three kittens. The mother was orange and white, making a rather partisan statement amidst the green, but her kittens were a confused mixture of colours. One was tortoiseshell, another orange, the third, and smallest, a tiny blur of black fur.

Ernie bent down and picked several of them up in his large but gentle hands, rather as an expert butcher casually yet lovingly handles prime steak. Unlike a butcher, Ernie then placed his valued handful on top of his head. Soon his head and shoulders were swathed with cats, startled but not displeased to discover themselves upon the grizzled eminence. Ernie beamed; the cats purred.

The cats are allowed to rove free about the farm. Although they are kept to kill mice and rats, a duty they perform with joyful diligence, they are also welcome in the house. 'They get well spoiled,' admits Ernie, but adds that they sleep in the barn.

I asked Ernie what the cats were called. He said that he didn't give them names but doubtless they had names for each other. It is a happy thought. One wonders what they call him.

# Mary

Carmen Callil has a cat called Mary. 'I called her Mary after Mary Wollstonecraft, because I thought she was going to have a difficult life. And I was right.' It seems not inapposite that the dynamic founder of Virago Books (and the current Managing Director of Chatto & Windus) should name her cat after the unhappy but courageous author of *The Vindication of the Rights of Women*, so it comes as something of a surprise to find that the said Mary is a thoroughly uncourageous ball of silver-streaked fluff and that Carmen addresses her as 'Pussl' ('the German for Pussy, I think'). Nevertheless it is indisputable that Pussl – or Mary – has had a difficult life.

Although it is a trite notion to blame the difficulties of the child on the attitudes of the parents, it seems that Mary's parents cannot be wholly exempted from responsibility. Mary comes from a theatrical family. Her father appears in advertisements for Kosset carpets while her mother promotes a brand of cat food. They can be seen on posters. Carmen suspects that the cameo Persian breed, to which Mary and her parents belong, was developed especially to provide cats for ads. Certainly the cameo's mix of silver-tabby and Persian produces cats of rare and rich beauty. Mary is no exception, with her silver-pointed ear-tufts, wide pale eyes and splendid harem-trousers.

Great beauty coupled with the instability of a theatrical background is, however, a combination unlikely to produce a level temper. It has not produced one in Liza Minnelli and it has not produced one in Mary. Moreover Mary is daft: 'The cat with no brain,' as Carmen puts it. But if Mary was blessed at birth with beauty, stupidity and nerves, the events of her upbringing have only served to compound these traits.

Carmen already had two cats – sisters called William and John – which she had been given by Germaine Greer, when she saw Mary in the window of the Palace Gate Pet Shop and felt that she must possess this gorgeous package of platinum fluff. William and John were not very impressed with the new arrival. 'They were highly intelligent cats. They were half Siamese and half alley cat, and maybe half Russian Blue as well,' says Carmen with a fine disregard for the niceties of mathematics but with a due appreciation of her cats' hybrid vigour.

William and John gave Mary a very hard time. They had already established their own territories and they refused to allow Mary into certain rooms. 'The combination of persecution and no brain

turned Mary into a whiner and a whinger.' From her part-Siamese
persecutors she learnt to scream (Siamese cats are the most vocal).
Now she wails in the night, 'which I could well do without,'
Carmen remarks. 'And when I take her to the vet she screams all
the way there and all the way back. So I don't take her often.'

This suits Mary as she is not an adventurous cat; the prospect of
travel and discovery does not set her whiskers abristle with
pleasure. Throughout the whole of Carmen's spacious book-lined
house there are only five places where she ventures. Her favourite
retreat is amongst the tattered hessian under Carmen's bed. When
the sun appears she removes to the ledge by the bedroom window.
Downstairs she has her own apartment suite, a ventilated
cupboard, with a cat-flap, which houses her litter tray and food
bowls. She will also follow the sun to a window at the back of the
drawing-room, where there is a comfortably upholstered chest on
which she can lounge. At night she returns to Carmen's bedroom

and, between noisy bouts of wailing, she lies on Carmen's nose.

Mary is obviously very attached to Carmen, although the attachment is fuelled more by vanity and timorousness than any nobler sentiments. Mary loves to be admired and protected, not the female virtues one most associates with viragos. 'Poor Mary, she's not intelligent, she's not a friend, really,' says Carmen. 'But she does have marvellous legs. She sits down and puts one foot in front of the other. She's like a painting.'

'I once tried to breed her properly because she is so beautiful,' says Carmen. The undertaking was not a success. After several frigid days down at the cattery being urged on by a bossy woman in a tweed jacket, Mary had still failed to 'perform'. The bossy woman in the tweed jacket rang for Carmen to collect her hopeless cat telling her, 'Your cat refuses to breed because it's in love with you.' 'I have a lesbian cat,' says Carmen, not without pride.

In recognition of Mary's touching though largely unrequited passion, and also as a penance for subjecting Mary to such a traumatic kittenhood, Carmen refuses to introduce any more animals into the house. Since William and John died about one and half a year ago respectively, Mary has been enjoying the pleasures of solitude, free from the persecuting paws of these more robust and intelligent felines. Carmen had wondered about getting a kitten to keep Mary company but decided that it would almost certainly upset either Mary or the kitten. At thirteen, Mary has become quite set in her ways. 'She's going to have just me for the rest of her natural life,' says Carmen. Mary looks much pleased with the prospect. Carmen is less sure.

As Mary stares wistfully up at her beloved owner, a timorous, wide-eyed, dumb blonde, Carmen returns the look with her own keen yet affectionate glare and pronounces, 'That cat is not easy to live with.'

# Beerbohm, Fleur, Janet, Whisky & Fudge

One of the charms of London's West End is its mixture of the smart and the seedy, the rough and the smooth. The colourful jungle of Soho's narrow streets gives way to the spacious boulevards of Piccadilly, the sober gaiety of Mayfair surrounds the inebriate jollity of Shepherd Market. Cats, canny and adaptable, are to be found throughout this heterogeneous square mile – low-life moggs and performing pussies rub shoulders with plump toff-cats.

One of the capital's foremost feline characters is Beerbohm, the sleek and handsome tabby at the Globe Theatre in Shaftesbury Avenue. He takes his name from Herbert Beerbohm Tree, the famous actor-manager at Her Majesty's, the theatre where Beerbohm (the cat) was born and brought up, before transferring to the Globe a decade ago. Beerbohm has much of the fabled charisma and vitality of his namesake, as well as an impeccably pressed fur costume in brown and black motley.

He is active at every level of the theatre. He lives below stage, looked after by Tony the carpenter, but is a frequent visitor to the actors' dressing-rooms, paying compliments to the leading ladies, bantering with the men and bolstering the confidence of tender hopefuls. Beerbohm addresses them without affectation as a fellow thespian. He has made several stage appearances, receiving particularly good notices for his unscheduled entrance during the Hinge and Bracket season. He was, however, mildly put out when the popularity of *Daisy Pulls It Off* led to extra evening performances; Beerbohm had appropriated the stage-set sofa as his bed and was obliged to delay his night's rest. Not that Beerbohm was surprised by the success of the show. Auditions and rehearsals are often graced with his presence; he likes to ensure that standards are maintained.

Beerbohm has many friends in the neighbourhood. Fleur, the elegant but shy cat at the nearby Lyric Theatre, prefers to loiter in the domestic cosiness of her own green room or amongst the luxuriant tresses in the wig department on the top floor of the building, than to swop theatrical gossip.

Until recently Beerbohm's favourite drinking companion was the portly black and white mogg called Boss Cat who lived across the way from the stage door on the counter of Hill & Co, ironmongers, in Rupert Street. Sadly Boss Cat has passed on, but two of his brothers still live in one of the small alleys off the street, looked after by the market-stall holders. They continue to be impressed by Beerbohm's tales of the limelight.

Less sociable is Janet, the formidable black and white *grande dame* in the Fratelli Camisa delicatessen at the foot of Berwick Street. Janet is large and nineteen years old. Until about six years ago she shared her home among the pendulous salamis and vast Parmesan cheeses with a sister, now dead. They arrived together as two black and white kittens from the RSPCA but, while Janet showed a keen interest in food and a dramatic propensity for growth, her sister was more restrained and never grew to anything more than half Janet's size.

They never received formal names but were always referred to as Big Puss and Little Puss (as in Big Ben and Little Dorrit rather than Big O and Little John). Nevertheless, the frequent inquiries by admiring customers prompted Ennio Camisa, the father of the business, to call them Janet and John.

Janet now lives an enviable life of long siestas and frequent meals. Although she is well fed on raw meat from the butcher's across the street and pasta from the family table, she still has an appetite for her favourite dish – freshly killed London pigeon. She catches them amongst the market stalls in the street and then kills them in the shop. 'It can cause a bit of an upset,' says Francesco Camisa, 'especially with women customers.'

Janet also presumes upon the good-will of the customers by eating the spinach leaves out of their overflowing carrier-bags. Although she consents to be stroked, she does not like to be fussed over and will curtail any gushing advance with a muffled swipe of her hefty paw. She is good with children but cannot abide other cats and detests dogs. She is currently engaged in a feud with a market-trader's Jack Russell. Janet sits on the threshold of the shop taunting the unwelcome terrier.

Whisky is untroubled by the dogs he encounters on his afternoon strolls in Green Park. Whisky is the very smart cat who lives in the bar at the delightfully secluded Stafford Hotel just off St James's. He was called in, along with his late sister Soda, ten years ago when construction work on the Underground system was prompting a lot of mice to seek alternative accommodation above ground. Whisky and Soda turned the rodent tide away from the revolving doors of the Stafford with the polite firmness common in the staff of the best hotels (and rare everywhere else).

The alarm over, Whisky now devotes himself to the pleasurable but no less serious business of helping Charles the barman mix drinks for the hotel guests. Dressed as for dinner in white tie and black tail, Whisky has the air (and figure) of a cat who lives well.

Across the well-tended acres of Green Park, on the other side of Piccadilly, resides another finely turned out feline, Fudge the cat at the In and Out Club. Although the In and Out (or, more properly, the Naval and Military) was founded as a services club, Fudge does not have a very martial bearing. Her luxuriant tabby coat is more

suggestive of an elaborate dress uniform than a set of combat fatigues. Her duties too seem to be more ornamental than functional. In her younger days (she is now fifteen) she would catch mice. Indeed she was so successful that the mouse population has now moved elsewhere.

She spends her afternoons on sentry duty, perched on one of the more comfortable arm chairs in the club smoking-room. Each evening, at a few moments before six, she comes to attention, makes a brisk parade around the smoking-room and then marches purposefully to the bar. She sits on one of the stools, eating crisps and listening amusedly to the tall tales of the club members. She has heard these tales often. But the familiarity of old friends, old stories and old surroundings is one of the pleasures of clubland.

Serenity and stillness are two of the foremost feline virtues. They are precious anywhere, but how very welcome it is to encounter them amidst the headlong bustle of the metropolis.

# Tabriz & Nevsky

Simon Playle has a passion for animals and the exotic. His flat in Fulham is a delightfully unexpected menagerie comprising two parrots, an iguana, a fleet of rare tortoises and two elegant cats – an Abyssinian and a Russian Blue. Simon's love of oriental refinement extends beyond his choice of cats to the decoration of his home and the strength of his interior design business. His eastern and feline interests often converge; two old and striking Ceylonese lions grace his fireside, and he does a brisk trade in Chinese pictures of cats and butterflies (a pictographic rendering of the Chinese word for happiness).

Simon has always lived amongst cats. He was brought up with a score of them in a large house in Suffolk. Even more influential were the years spent attending an engagingly dotty prep school nearby. The place was run by two cat-mad brothers and their cat-mad sister. The regime was a liberal one; the triumvirate was addressed by their Christian names and the feline virtues of independence and courtesy were highly regarded. There was plenty of instruction to be got in the said virtues as the house was full of virtuous cats and the walls thick with pictures of exemplary felines. The living cats boasted formal yet playful monikers such as Mrs Toast, Mr Cotton and Mr Claw, in accordance with their habits and foibles.

Who would not blossom in such surroundings? Simon's love of cats and flair for design budded and blossomed in the congenial atmosphere. He was even commissioned to paint two cats on the shutters of one of the schoolrooms.

Simon's own taste in cats runs to the exotic. 'I like unusual things,' he explains. 'I prefer foreign cats to British moggs. I don't like fat, blocky English cats.' His two cats, Nevsky and Tabriz, are the antithesis of fat and blocky (and English, come to that).

Nevsky is a distinguished Russian Blue. At fourteen he has the unforced yet aristocratic dignity that one might expect of a cat whose forebears provided hat-fur for the Tsars. He is no Bolshevik – but then, he came from Harrods. He arrived as a tiny, 'frosted kitten' and, although some of the frost has now melted from his blue-grey coat, his looks would still grace a Russian steppe as handsomely as they do a Fulham doorstep. Like many Russians (when sober), Nevsky is quiet and not easily perturbed.

In recent years, however, he has been rejuvenated by the presence of Tabriz. Tabriz (named after a favourite fabric design) is a sleek and forceful Abyssinian cat. She is three years old.

Abyssinian cats are the direct descendants of the Ancient Egyptian felines, their colouring has the natural tone of a golden hare and their sinewy curves and tall ears recall the Egyptian statuettes in the British Museum. A whiff of mystery surrounds any Abyssinian cat, and Tabriz makes little effort to dispel the aura. The very manner of her arrival was mysterious.

Before Tabriz Simon had another Abyssinian, called Balkis. Balkis was hit by a car and, despite the ministrations of the Blue Cross, died. Simon tried to replace Balkis immediately but Abyssinians in Britain are a small breed, made smaller by the recent ravages of feline leukaemia, and there were no kittens available. Distressed, Simon began to consider alternatives. But before he could settle upon a second choice the Abyssinian Cat Association rang to ask whether he would be interested in taking on a young but adult Abyssinian recently found abandoned in Putney. The best efforts of the Police and RSPCA had been unable to locate its former owners, so a new home was being sought.

Simon accepted the offer gratefully, although, as any cat-lover would have been, he was a mite anxious about accepting a grown-up and probably distraught cat into a harmonious household of parrots and tortoises, presided over by an elderly Russian cat confirmed in his habits and conservative in his disposition.

He collected the abandoned Abyssinian from the local RSPCA and was curious to note that it had been brought into care on the day of Balkis' death. His curiosity was further aroused when, on arrival at the flat, this rescued stray strode confidently over the threshold and inspected each room as though it was both friendly and familiar. The young cat was unfazed by the parrots, charmed by and charming to the dignified Nevsky. Indeed she behaved in every particular as though she had merely returned home after a brief holiday rather than arrived at a strange house after a traumatic ordeal. 'It was as if she had always lived here,' recalls Simon.

Why Tabriz should have abandoned her former home or why it should have abandoned her remains a mystery. But, though for the most part she wears a playful and domestic mask, the feral instincts of her ancestors still linger in her blood. The week after I had called on her, she disappeared. She was gone for over a week. Simon despaired of her. But she returned one night, thin and bedraggled and, more curiously, sporting several ticks. She had obviously been living rough in wild terrain. But where and why? Had she been celebrating arcane and ancient rites in the wastes of Brompton Cemetry? Or mixing with ne'er-do-well moggs from the wrong side of the railway tracks? Tabriz, happy to be home, yet unruffled by her strange excursion, refuses to reveal her secrets.

Though thin, Tabriz had survived happily away from the catfood tin. She is, even when at home, a good hunter and a better thief. She brings back bones from the neighbouring gardens much to the consternation of the local dogs and the amusement of Nevsky.

Nevsky and Tabriz have continued to get on well. Nevsky enjoys his playful young companion and Tabriz respects his senior's indolence, looking after him and washing behind his ears with touching consideration.

Harmony prevails amongst the house's living creatures. 'The cats even quite like the parrots,' says Simon. 'There has never been a contretemps, thank goodness. I believe in giving animals a bit of tension in their lives. If you give them everything on a plate they have less character.' Tabriz and Nevsky, sharing a stolen bone, cannot but agree.

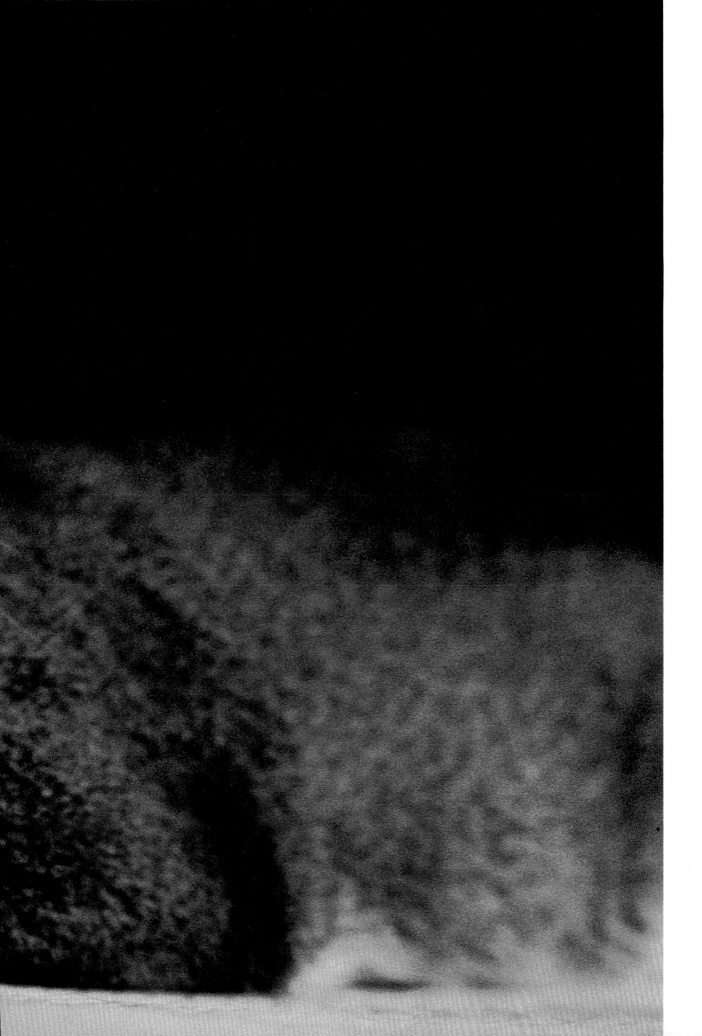

# Tiddles

Cats have long stalked in the groves of academe. By doing very little they have managed to suggest that they are, perhaps, intellectuals. Certainly cats appeal to the intellectual temperament: from Newton and Bentham to E. P. Thompson and Germaine Greer, questing minds have sought and valued feline companionship. Cats are, of course, proverbially curious. But while intellectuals might account curiosity a virtue the proverb scarcely recommends it – at least as far as cats are concerned. Perhaps it is the cat's predeliction for sedentary calm that strikes a chord with the philosophic spirit. Or maybe the feline capacity for in-fighting and brawling appeals to the cloistered academic.

Oxford colleges, recognising these many links between the feline and the donnish temper, have always tolerated cats. Dogs, however, for all their doggish charm being essentially philistine, are less well received. Indeed Harry Pitt, a don at Worcester College, was obliged to have his dog officially declared a cat so that he could continue to keep it in his rooms. Amongst the many Oxford colleges few provide an apter setting for feline grace than St Catherine's, known as St Cats.

Tiddles is the St Cats' cat. Tiddles belongs to the Master of the college, Sir Patrick Nairne. There is some debate as to whether the Master or his cat has more influence over the running of the college. Certainly the influence of Tiddles over the ambience of the place should not be underestimated. He is involved with college activities at all levels, and is held in equal affection by Senior Common Room and undergraduates.

He insisted on appearing in the most recent of Fellows' photographs, waiting for all the dons to take up their positions before sauntering to the front of the line-up and posing shamelessly for the camera. When, however, the photographer attempted to arrange Tiddles' position for one of the shots, the cat stalked over to the camera and wrapped himself around the legs of the tripod.

Tiddles is not only a self-appointed fellow; he is also an honorary member of both the J.C.R. and the graduate common room. It is a measure of Tiddles' natural authority – as well as a happy reflection of the perceptive imagination of at least some elements within the college – that the cat has been put up for the presidency of both institutions. Sadly, however, he missed both posts by a whisker, as is so often the way with cats.

As with many great and bold spirits who have been denied the high office they perhaps deserved (one thinks of Sidney Smith,

Julian Critchley, and Brian Clough), Tiddles is unmarred by bitterness. Indeed he bears all the signs of an existence of good humour and good living. Sir Patrick's daughter remarked on a recent visit home that, 'Tiddles is getting fat – like the dons.' Both Tiddles and the dons affected not to hear. A more diplomatic soul might have suggested that Tiddles was merely well-built.

Moreover, his chief glory is not his stately tabby flank but his handsome face. 'He has an extraordinarily nice face,' says Sir Patrick with justifiable pride. A lively kindness dances in the cat's green eyes, and the trim white beard lends him a dignity much in keeping with his setting.

Tiddles, like many cats and most dons, does not suffer fools lightly, nor does he tolerate careless behaviour. 'I have always admired that genius Beatrix Potter,' says Sir Patrick, 'when she writes that Tabitha Twitchet was "affronted".' It is such an apt word for a cat put out of countenance. 'If Tiddles is accidentally shut in a room overnight, when she is let out in the morning she is very affronted. She refuses food and kind words. She will jump up on to the window-sill by the sink and eat the last geranium.'

Tiddles likes flowers, not only to eat but also to sniff at and loll about in. She is fortunate in the gardens of St Cats. No other college was designed to be so much a part of its own gardens. The architect, Arne Jacobsen, mapped out the planting of the grounds with the same meticulous care that he devoted to every other detail of the

college, from the airy vastness of the dining hall to the specially-fashioned left-handed soup-spoons.

There are, of course, other delights in the gardens besides the flowers. An anxious ichthyologist in the MCR has accused Tiddles of poaching goldfish out of the moat, and the Dean, an eminent zoologist, fears that the cat is carrying off moorhen chicks from their nests along the river bank. Sir Patrick defends his cat against such slanders. It seems likely that there is another culprit. Lady Nairne has seen Tiddles sitting up in a tree taunting a large fox as it stalked the infant moorhens.

The cat has the run of the college buildings as well as the college gardens. He once appeared at High Table, but prefers the more informal banter of the kitchen. He also makes free use of the students' rooms. The undergraduates are particularly pleased to be singled out for the special favour of a visit. One student cited Tiddles' kindly concern for her as one of the important and abiding pleasures of her time at Oxford. Not all visitors, however, are so charmed. A South American conference delegate who was staying in the college during the vacation, was discovered one morning screaming in the corridor, dressed in her nightie. She was convinced that a leopard was trying to get in through her bedroom window. A chivalrous fellow delegate went to her rescue and discovered Tiddles tapping benignly on the woman's windowpane and some very thick spectacles on the woman's dressing-table.

Tiddles seldom leaves the confines of the college. His relations with the town cats are strained. There have, alas, been some unpleasant town v. gown incidents. One woman was convinced that Tiddles was terrorising her cats, and went so far as to throw a bucket of water over him. Tiddles was most affronted. He has made an occasional visit to Magdalen. The stroll down Addison's Walk is a pleasant one and the Porter's Lodge at Magdalen is always kept warm. On arrival, Tiddles presents himself at the Lodge and the Porter, reading the cat's name and telephone number off the medallion round its neck, calls for Sir Patrick to come and collect his charge.

To be able to combine a charming afternoon walk, a cosy resting-place and the sight of your own (and St Catherine's) Master having to play the part of a chauffeur, is the work of a mind worthy of the great university.